Apples of Gold
In Settings of Silver

By Barbara McCormick and Lin Artus

Kingdom Publishers

Apples of Gold in Settings of Silver
Copyright© Linda Artus and Barbara McCormick

All rights reserved. No part of this book may be
reproduced in any form by photocopying or any
electronic or mechanical means, including information
storage or retrieval systems, without permission in
writing from both the copyright owner and the publisher
of the book. The right of Linda Artus and Barbara McCormick to be
identified as the authors of this work has been asserted by them in
accordance with the Copyright, Designs and Patents Act
1988 and any subsequent amendments thereto.
A catalogue record for this book is available from the
British Library.

All Scripture Quotations have been taken from the New American Standard of the Bible.

ISBN: 978-1-911697-18-3

1st Edition by Kingdom Publishers

Kingdom Publishers
London, UK.

You can purchase copies of this book from any leading bookstore or
email **contact@kingdompublishers.co.uk**

Contents

Chapter 1	A Bride Prepared	9
Chapter 2	A Bride's Response	19
Chapter 3	Banana Skins	26
Chapter 4	Tangled ropes	33
Chapter 5	Coping with Crisis	45
Chapter 6	Wooed by the World	52
Chapter 7	Enemy of our Lives	62
Chapter 8	Deception of God's Children	74
Chapter 9	Defence for the Warfare with Satan	84
Chapter 10	Enemy Opportunities	93
Chapter 11	Squatters in the House	99
Chapter 12	Judgement Cometh	103

Preface

This book, though small in volume, has come as a result of nearly twenty years of weekly praying together and seeking the Lord. On those special occasions, He gave us passages of Scripture to study. The Lord directed us to write down what we learned. Eventually this period of time seemed to come to an end, as we were no longer receiving material to research from the Lord. We earnestly sought the Lord as to what to do next.

His answer came in the form of a vision in which a field of golden wheat lay cut and ready to be harvested. At the same time we were reminded of the feeding of the five thousand, where Jesus commanded the disciples, "You give them something to eat."   God provided the food, but the disciples gave it out to the multitudes. (Matthew 14:16-19)

So from all that our Lord provided, we made the bread and wrote this book.

It may be uncomfortable reading at times, as its contents reveal the backslidden nature of compromised and deceived Christianity.

We hope and pray that you hear God speak to you through its pages, and that it will make a difference for good in your life, and whatever is ahead for us all, we will be truly ready and waiting for our Bridegroom's return….. the second coming of our Lord Jesus Christ.

This book is suitable for individual bible study.

All Bible quotations are from the New American Standard Version unless otherwise indicated.

Chapter 1

A Bride Prepared

"Let us rejoice and be glad and give the glory to Him, for the marriage of the Lamb has come and His bride has made herself ready." (Revelation 19:7)

The bride in this verse represents the Church in heaven, when the bridegroom Jesus, comes to take His bride, to the marriage supper of the Lamb. She is ready and arrayed in righteousness.

However, Jesus told His followers while they are on earth to be ready at all times as they do not know the hour of His coming. At the moment the Church is decidedly unprepared and far from ready for the coming of her Lord.

- There is compromise in the name of Love but without truth.
- There is the neglect of reading and living by God's word.
- There is the mixture of the unholy with the counterfeit.

The two of us looked at the current state of the Church. These things distressed us greatly. We wanted to pray effectively. We wanted to cry, but we couldn't! We were aware of a cold, distant feeling of apathy about the whole thing, and we didn't know why?

It seemed our feelings reflected the general attitude of much of the Church in this part of the world.

We earnestly sought God over the matter to find out what He wanted us do.

God provided the answer in the nuggets of gold He enabled us to dig out of His word.

In times past, God always gave very precise instructions about how His house was to be constructed, these plans have far transcended man's highest thoughts. God requires the same in the building of His Church. All too often today much of this is man-inspired. It is a pointless exercise to think we can achieve anything without God's direction.

In Isaiah 66 we read about the attitudes of heart and mind God requires of those whom He will use.

God said, "To this one I will look, to him who is humble and contrite of spirit and who trembles at My word." (Isaiah 66:2b)

What is your understanding of this scripture?

....

....

....

A definition of humility:

Lowliness of heart,
Knowing and understanding our weaknesses,
Happy to be of no account,
Happy to be a servant,
Pliant, submissive,
Unpretentious

In Philippians 2:1-8 we are encouraged to maintain love in our fellowship with each other, to be affectionate, compassionate, and united in spirit, embracing the concept of humility, whilst selflessly caring for our Christian family. We are to be like Jesus, who emptied Himself of His greatness, in order to show us how to live, coming in the form of a servant, and being fully dependant on His Father to do His will.

We prove ourselves to be blameless and innocent when we are obedient to God's word, and fully submitted to Him and His direction for our lives. (Philippians 2:15-16)

How do you feel and respond when you are asked to submit to the wishes of another you disagree with, in order to keep the peace?

....

....

....

In what sort of circumstances might you find it difficult to put others first and yourself last?

....

....

....

Humility is summed up when we have the attitude of mind that says, "Thy will, not mine be done."

Isaiah also tells us we need to be 'contrite in spirit'.

(Isaiah 66:2b)

This is the recognition of ourselves as sinners before Almighty God, and our own inability to do anything about it.

In the parable Jesus told, He illustrated this point to those who thought they were righteous. Read Luke 18:9-14

Who do you identify most with, the tax-collector or the Pharisee?

....

Why? ....

....

Isaiah stated that our righteous deeds are like a filthy garment. (Isaiah 64:6)

What do we understand this to mean?

....

....

It is only in Christ that our sins are now covered and paid for by His blood shed on the cross.

The contrite in heart accept that apart from God they can do nothing that is up to His standard.

Contrition is knowing that the vileness of sin is still inherent within us, even when we think we are doing well.

Paul felt just like this as he wrote Romans 7:14-25.

He said, "Wretched man that I am who will set me free from the body of this death?"

Our old nature does not improve with age.

How do you view yourself regarding your sinful nature?

....

....

The third and final criteria Isaiah gives to those who would walk closely with God, is that they should 'tremble at His word'. (Isaiah 66:2b)

To "fear and tremble" means to be:

- Reverent, in awe of God.
- Afraid, lest we fall into sin. (Philippians 2:12-13)

The children of Israel trembled at the terrifying scene which accompanied the presence of an awesome and almighty God when Moses went up Mount Sinai to receive the Law. (Exodus 20:18)

Moses said to the people, "Do not be afraid; for God has come in order to test you, and in order that the fear of Him may remain with you, so that you may not sin." (Exodus 20:20)

How do we who have experienced the grace of God, differentiate between being afraid of God and the fear of God regarding our sin?

....

....

If we tremble at God's word we will hear and obey.

"But to this one I will look, to him who is humble and contrite of spirit, and who trembles at My word." (Isaiah 66:2b)

We looked at this verse and considered if it was true of us.

Do you consider the seriousness of taking God's word lightly?

....

....

This is a foundational verse for all who truly seek to obey the Lord.

The following verse was shocking to us. We had not realized how God actually views the sin of hypocrisy in His people.

"But he who kills an ox is like one who slays a man."
(Isaiah 66:3)

God required a young bullock to be offered in the sacrificial ceremony to Him. The ox that was offered here was an old beast, showing a complete lack of repentance, and a detachment from practical holiness.

This was so totally offensive, that in God's eyes this was like the crime of killing a man in cold blood.

Although these offerings are no longer expected of God's children, if we are serious and godly in our consideration of the mercies of God we should offer our lives as Paul calls us to.

"I urge you therefore, brethren, by the mercies of God, to present your bodies a living and holy sacrifice, acceptable to God, which is your spiritual service of worship." (Romans 12:1)

For something to be sacrificial it costs us something.

What sacrifices does God require of you?

....

....

Do you give your prime young bullock in these matters, or is your offering 'past its sell by date'?

Seriously consider how you serve the Lord in these matters.

"He who sacrifices a lamb is like the one who breaks a dog's neck." (Isaiah 66:3)

A man would sacrifice a lamb in order to say sorry to God for sins he had committed. If he was not truly penitent but just going through the motions, then it was as offensive to God as offering an unclean animal like a dog. These animals were considered to be lowest of the low, not only this, but they were considered to be an expression of utter contempt. (Matthew 15:26) Dogs were even used as a synonym for the wicked. (Psalm 22:16)

The whole point of sacrificing a specified clean animal was to make atonement with its blood. However, to the impenitent, who were religiously observant, but devoid of holiness, it was as if a blasphemous offering was made by breaking the neck of an abominable animal, which revealed the offeror's true state of heart, as well as the fact that its death produced no blood. This therefore offered no benefit at all to the supplicant and went no way to placating God's wrath at this sin.

For the Christian, there is no place for hypocrisy. Just being religiously observant is not enough. We must choose to live a life of holiness. To repent is to choose to turn away from sin and walk in the opposite direction.

"But if we walk in the light as He Himself is in the light...and the blood of Jesus His Son cleanses us from all sin." (1 John 1:7)

How do you personally define true repentance?

....

....

How do you consider the sin of hypocrisy?

....

....

"He who offers a grain offering is like one who offers swine's blood." (Isaiah 66:3)

The purpose of a grain offering (cereal or bread) was that it was to be given as a gift to God, often to say thank you to Him for benefits given. But to the unrepentant people of Israel who offered it without true thankfulness it was as if they had offered God swine's blood. A swine (pig) was an unclean animal, not fit for use by God, indeed the Hebrews were to consider pigs as abhorrent in every context. So, to offer its blood was an abominable insult to holy God.

Since Jesus' work of atonement, does God still think of a believer's sins in the same way? (Hebrews 10:10-18)

....

Why/Why not? ....

Are we still responsible if our offering is contemptible?

....

Today we say thank you to God through the offerings of ourselves, our time, and our money.

What specific sacrifices do you offer to God?

....

....

How might our offerings be offensive to God?

....

....

....

Even though our sin, guilt and condemnation were dealt with at the cross, Paul makes it very clear that the way we have lived our lives and the results of our works will be seen and will be judged. (1 Corinthians 3:11-15)

"He who burns incense is like one who blesses an idol."

Incense was meant to be burnt before the Lord as a way of saying thank you. But when this offering was brought with a heart that was far from God, then God compared this to blessing an idol. The Hebrew word for 'idol', used by Isaiah, means activity, which is empty and vain, which has no purpose in the divine scheme of things. It refers to those things which would deceive us into thinking that there is great point to what we do, and that it will bring us benefit, when in actual fact, it is a worthless pursuit. And we do not realize the dangers therein.

To 'bless an idol' is to believe that the ways **WE** choose and delight in, as opposed to God's ways, are the correct ways, and are acceptable to God. However, if studied closely, we find these ways are vain, empty, self-centred, and fruitless and unacceptable to God.

Can you identify any of these idols in your life or in the Church?

....

....

The things which we may think are mildly offensive to God, are in truth, abhorrent to Him.

After we had studied these verses at great length, we came to the conclusion that it is not possible to pray for the Church without true humility, and that we should all realize that we are poor in spirit and utterly dependant on God and His word to help and guide us. Then we will understand what He requires of us.

Chapter 2

A Bride's Response

What hinders our understanding of God's word?

Behold, a preacher went out to preach, as led by the Holy Spirit. He preached the word of God to believers and some understood and some did not. Those who understood knew what response God expected from them, and they obediently put into practice what they had learnt. Those who did not understand what the preacher was saying were not able to respond.

Why do you think some Christians in the Church may not understand the word of God that is preached to them?

....

....

See these Scripture verses for different examples of where understanding failed.

- Proverbs 18:2

    Understanding does not always come immediately, it must be sought. It must be wanted. The writer of Proverbs tells us that a foolish man will not be interested in seeking true understanding, but rather he prefers to reveal to others what's on his own mind. This is like a believer who thinks his own interpretations of a matter are right, and therefore he is not open to be proved wrong. This foolish attitude will prevent truth and understanding from ministering to us, which is why it is essential that we be prepared to truly listen to what others have to say especially if they are questioning something we do or believe. We should always bring our views to God for affirmation.

How often do you rely on your own understanding and interpretation, of a spiritual matter without checking it with the word of God?

....

How open are you to being corrected and truly listening to what others have to say about spiritual matters you disagree on?

....

- Mark 8:14-21

    The disciples were not listening to what Jesus was talking about when He warned of the 'leaven of the Pharisees' and the leaven of Herod'. Leaven in the Bible is symbolic of an insidious type of evil which spreads slowly and quietly and affects everything it touches. This could be hypocrisy, ritualism, self- righteousness and tradition. Herod's leaven could be his scepticism, immorality and worldliness.

    However, they had completely missed the point because all they could think about was the bread they had forgotten to bring. Jesus began to chide them for their lack of faith in Him to provide for them, considering He had just performed two miracles in which He had provided bread for thousands of people from virtually nothing.

    The disciples were thinking in worldly terms, whereas Christ wanted them to think in spiritual terms. The Scriptures tell us that the disciples "had not gained any insight from the incident of the loaves, for their hearts were hardened" (Mark 6:52). Jesus was saying that the hearts of His disciples were dull and insensitive, and unable to perceive the spiritual message the feeding of the thousands was meant to teach them. They could only see through their natural eyes that they had no bread, and it did not occur to them that Jesus could remedy the situation with a word.

This is like believers who know that Jesus can perform miracles, but they do not yet perceive things spiritually, and fail to look beyond their own needs to Christ, and the possibility of supernatural intervention, because they are so absorbed in their own natural way of doing things.

Do you find it hard to look beyond your own solutions to a problem?

....

....

How easily do you remember that God wants to be involved in that problem, possibly in a supernatural way?

....

....

- Luke 24:13-31

    The disciples on the Emmaus Road were sad because they had lost hope in Jesus. As far as they were concerned, He had died on the cross, end of story. Their misunderstanding began because they had wrong expectations of Christ. When He spoke about 'redeeming Israel', they thought He meant that He was going to raise an army and defeat the Romans. Even though there were reports of an empty tomb, they would not believe because of their own wrong, sad reflections of the situation. In fact Christ's resurrection had overcome far more than just the physical redemption of Israel. He had redeemed the whole world from the power of sin.

How might our own misconceptions prevent us from clearly seeing God's plan and purpose for our lives?

....

....

In what ways can having false expectations about future events be dangerous to us? e.g. not understanding or misunderstanding what is prophesied to happen.

....

....

The evening of the day Christ was resurrected, the disciples were having difficulty in accepting the news that eyewitnesses had seen the risen Christ. They did not quickly accept without reservation all they had heard from Jerusalem, even though it had all been prophesied throughout Scripture and shown to be necessary that Christ should suffer these things before He entered His glory. Jesus said to them, "O foolish men, and slow of heart (meaning not recognising or comprehending divine things) to believe in all that the prophets have spoken!" v.25.

It is essential that we believe and learn from what the prophets have taught us. All that is predicted in both the Old Testament and the New Testament was inspired by God to give us insight into all that will happen in the future.

Like these disciples, we believers can get despondent if we fail to understand, from God's perspective, the distressing circumstances we may find ourselves in as Christians, especially if we don't have knowledge of, or discern all that is foretold us in the Bible. We have much to discover about Jesus' first and second coming, and all that God seeks to do in human history, from prophetic teaching.

We can believe all that the prophets have spoken. All that has not already come to pass, will do.

Do you seek to study and understand such things?

....

....

What problems may we encounter if we disregard prophetic witness? (e.g. 2 Peter 3:3-4)

....

....

There are those who tell us that prophecy is not important or necessary any more. We are indeed foolish if we listen to their teaching.

- John 20:24-29

    Thomas wanted concrete proof that Christ had risen from the dead, even though Christ had told the disciples that they would see Him again (John 16:22). He was not prepared to accept the testimonies of his fellow disciples, who had seen Jesus alive already. He did not believe the truth of what the others had seen. His own human reasoning prevented Thomas from understanding what had happened, and therefore he doubted and would not believe. He needed to see for himself.

Some believers will hear the Word of God but before they are willing to accept it as truth, they need to see the proof of its validity for their own circumstances. However we are to walk by faith and not by sight. (2 Corinthians 5:7) Our Lord dealt graciously with faithless Thomas, but it is much better for those of us who have not seen, yet have believed, we are truly blessed.

Are there areas in your life of faith that you question and where you find it hard to believe?

....

....

Why is it essential that we, in this age, live by faith and not by sight?

....

....

In all of the scenarios mentioned above, the people failed to understand and see things from God's perspective.

In Proverbs 2:1-9 we learn the importance of receiving and treasuring God's Word. It will give us wisdom and understanding when we truly seek it. Do you cry out for discernment and understanding? Do you search to find the hidden treasures of wisdom, knowledge and understanding? There is much benefit from God if you do.

How do you respond when God specifically speaks to you through His word?

- Do you put it into action immediately?

- Do you write it down in order to retain what was said?

- Do you put it on hold until you are ready to deal with it?

- Other

God can speak to us in many and varied ways. A willingness to hear and obey God is essential and will bring us understanding of His word and what is expected of us.

If we do not act on what we have learned, there is a great danger of our heart becoming hardened. This can happen gradually. Each time we ignore the Spirit's promptings, we become a little more unteachable and resistant to the changes God would make in our lives.

We will now go on to consider the things that can potentially inhibit our individual walk with God, which, without care and attention may trip us up and cause us to fall.

Chapter 3

Banana Skins

One unseen banana skin can do a lot of damage when slipped upon. One unseen patch of spiritual darkness can bring a believer down.

The book of 2 Corinthians contains valuable insights given by Paul to the Corinthian Church. It is a collection of Paul's teaching regarding the outworking of the New Covenant in the Church. In these chapters he describes how to be conformed to the image of Christ by the Holy Spirit's glorious light that surpasses the fading glory of the Old Covenant (3:2-18). The following scriptures are taken from 2 Corinthians Chapters 4-8. They can be used by the believer to expose spiritual banana skins in their lives.

We have specifically considered the **negatives** of that which Paul teaches, in order to clarify the importance of avoiding these things. Reflect on each of the following.

- 4:1 Losing heart in any good work or service we do for God. (Luke 18:1; Galatians 6:9)

- 4:2 Not renouncing or disowning our past (not bringing our past to the Light), adulterating the Word of God, (e.g. mixing human tradition with the pure Word of the gospel, or adding to the Word of God even if unknowingly, and distorting Scripture e.g. by taking a verse out of context and using as a truth statement.)

- 4:5-7 Elevating ourselves rather than Christ in the ministries we are involved in, and therefore being the master instead of a servant. Failing to recognise that our power comes from God and not from ourselves.

- 4:8 Being afflicted in any way and crushed by it. Being so perplexed by problems and circumstances so that we end up in a state of despair.

- 4:9 Fearing persecution and that God might forsake us. Being cast down, and fearing death.

- 4:10 Not being willing or prepared to suffer even though we know God will use this to make His life manifest in us.

- 4:13 Having faith in God, but not having the courage of our convictions to speak out what we believe.

- 4:14-17 Not seeing God's good plans in the midst of suffering, and therefore losing heart when we experience the bad times.

- 4:18 Looking at what is seen (the temporal) rather than what is unseen (the spiritual)

Read 2 Corinthians 4:1-18, and explain how each of these verses can help a believer to overcome the negatives listed above?

....

....

....

....

Problems of 'keeping things to ourselves'

2 Corinthians

- 6:11 Keeping quiet, not speaking freely to others about the gospel, of having a closed heart - not willing to share the truth of God with others.

- 6:12 Being restrained by inward affections i.e. not being open to each other, but being hemmed in by sympathies to other things.

- 6:13 Not opening up to each other.

In what ways can keeping things to ourselves be harmful to us as Christians and beneficial to our enemy the devil?

....

....

Mixture with the world

- 6:14 Being partnered with non-believers in our work for God.

- 6:15 Of having more in common with unbelievers and so mixing with the world.

- 6:16 Being deceived into believing there can be agreement between God and the idols of this world.

- 6:17 The danger of not separating ourselves from this mixture, and therefore contaminating ourselves.

Read 2 Corinthians 6:14-17 and consider each verse. In what different areas of life are we to keep separate from the world?

....

....

....

What is God's solution to the problem? (v.17)

....

....

Not Keeping Spiritually Clean

- 7:1   Not walking in the promises in 6:17-18 by

    Not cleansing ourselves from all defilement of the flesh (all forms of physical impurity e.g. depravity, drunkenness etc.)

- Not cleansing ourselves from what we know to be wrong in our spirit by the power of God (e.g. anger, bitterness, anything that constitutes ungodliness).

How can having reverential fear or awe of God help us in the process of becoming holy?

....

....

....

Wrong thinking

- 7:2-3 Not opening our hearts to each other because we have misunderstood what has been spoken, and wrongly received it as condemnation.

  Paul's purpose was to instruct, not to condemn, (he was not pointing the finger at anyone in the congregation to say you are not doing this, but rather he was saying, this is what every believer needs to do if they are to be children of God.)

In what ways can our mistaking truth for condemnation, flag up something wrong in us?

....

....

What problems may we incur if we reject a person bringing God's word to us?

....

....

- 7:4 Losing confidence in the brethren: Such a leader may have certain expectations of his flock, but become disheartened, loose hope, and give up, when they fail to come up to the standard he wants them to achieve.

What would you say is the spiritual root of his problem?

....

....

- 7:5-7 The banana skin of not comforting, encouraging and supporting the brethren through their trials. Members should have the same care for one another, and if one member suffers, all the members suffer with them.

  (1 Corinthians 12:25-26)

- 7:8 Not being prepared to bring truth to an erring brother, (for fear of hurting them or any other reason).

- 7:9-10 The banana skin of making someone sorrowful for the wrong reasons, just to make them feel guilty or remorseful for what they have done, instead of having the intention of producing in them a godly sorrow with the purpose of bringing them to repentance.

- 7:11 The banana skin of not being truly sorry for the wrong we have done, only remorseful for the bitter harvest we have reaped from it.

Who suffers most when we do not fulfil what is required of us?

(1 Corinthians 12:12)

....

....

Self-centred service

- 8:1-4 The banana skin of giving with wrong motives, or grudgingly, or for what we will get out of it.

- 8:7 The banana skin of not abounding in faith, knowledge, diligence and love, and hence we can become shallow, half- hearted and discouraged believers. We lose the abundant power, joy and sense of God.

- 8:24 The danger of not providing proof of genuine love, and therefore not having a good reputation among the churches.

Taking a tumble can seriously knock our confidence and our faith.

Why is it important to return to Jesus as soon as possible after we have fallen into sin? (See Luke 22:31-34)

....

....

"Now for this very reason also, applying all diligence, in your faith supply moral excellence, and in your moral excellence, knowledge; and in your knowledge, self-control, and in your self-control, perseverance, and in your perseverance, godliness; and in your godliness, brotherly kindness, and in your brotherly kindness, love. For if these qualities are yours and are increasing, they render you neither useless nor unfruitful in the true knowledge of our Lord Jesus Christ. For he who lacks these qualities is blind or short-sighted, having forgotten his purification from his former sins. Therefore, brethren be all the more diligent to make certain about His calling and choosing you; for as long as you practice these things you will never stumble." (2 Peter 1:5-10)

Chapter 4

Tangled ropes

As a banana skin can trip up individuals, so tangled ropes can cause many, if not a whole congregation of believers to fall. There may be many such ropes in churches. The cultural thinking of the age can be such a stumbling block, adversely influencing some within the community, in subtle ways, which frequently result in dispute and division.

Psalm 133 speaks of the advantages and importance of fellowship and partnership, and ultimately the blessing that unity provides.

The problem of disunity (tangled ropes) within the church stops us from being the 'one' that Jesus prayed we would be. This can be a vicious circle of disagreement, disharmony and disbelief.

The Ground and Criteria of Unity:

The basic grounds of unity are having a real and active relationship with Jesus Christ and to believe that the Bible is the Word of God, and is the ultimate authority that we are to live by. (John 15:10)

Would you agree/ disagree? Why/ why not?

....

....

By definition, the ground of unity is that which unifies.

Often churches see unity in terms of agreement to certain doctrinal statements.

Creeds from the early Church Fathers establish and expand the basic doctrines that Paul states in Ephesians 3:4-6. "There is one body, one Spirit, one hope, one Lord, one faith, one baptism, and one God and Father of all." At root level these creeds state biblical truth accepted by most of the major denominations.

Read the Nicene Creed below and see if you think it is a sufficient basis for unity between churches?

We believe in one God,
the Father, the Almighty,
Maker of heaven and earth,
of all that is seen and unseen.
We believe in one Lord, Jesus Christ,
the only Son of God,
eternally begotten of the Father,
God from God, Light from Light,
true God from true God,
begotten, not made,
of one Being with the Father.
Through Him all things were made.
For us and for our salvation
He came down from heaven:
by the power of the Holy Spirit
He became incarnate from the Virgin Mary,
and was made man.
For our sake He was crucified under Pontius Pilate;
He suffered death and was buried.
On the third day He rose again

in accordance with the Scriptures;
He ascended into heaven
and is seated at the right hand of the Father.
He will come again in glory to judge the living and the dead,
and His kingdom will have no end.
We believe in the Holy Spirit, the Lord, the giver of life,
who proceeds from the Father and the Son.
With the Father and the Son He is worshipped and glorified.
He has spoken through the Prophets.
We believe in one holy catholic and apostolic Church.
We acknowledge one baptism for the forgiveness of sins.
We look for the resurrection of the dead,
and the life of the world to come. Amen.

Do you think creeds such as the Nicene Creed are a sufficient ground for unity?

....

....

Look more closely at the Nicene Creed. Do you agree with everything it states?

....

....

Problems with the Creed

- Can believing in a creed ensure that a person truly knows Christ, and abides in Him as opposed to knowing about Him?

....

....

- Can believing in a creed be sufficient to establish whether people fully believe in the atoning work of Christ?

....

....

Some churches, to all intents and purposes, give a biblical account of the workings of salvation, but then add man-made doctrines which question the efficacious nature of the Atonement.

- Can we distinguish from a basic set of beliefs (as in this creed) and use it as a basis for unity without taking into account the rest of what any particular church believes?

....

....

When a person states they believe in the Holy Spirit, this does not guarantee that what they believe is not counterfeit. For example, a person may believe that the Holy Spirit has directed them through a dream or vision, when the content of such is clearly opposed to the teachings of Scripture. "But the Spirit explicitly says in later times, some will fall away from the faith, paying attention to deceitful spirits and doctrines of demons." (1 Timothy 4:1)

Interpretations

Perhaps differences of opinion in interpretation of Scripture is a significant factor that leads to disunity. Look at the list below of some of the reasons why we have so many different interpretations.

- Interpretations come from denominational bias.

- Language – problems with translation. There are significant problems in translation; sometimes it is hard to find a word in one language which truly represents a word in another language. This has been the cause of serious division in the Church.

- Historical Background – what is the context: When we interpret the Scriptures, we must take into account the historical context. For example, in the time of Paul, a lady having short, cropped hair meant that she was a temple prostitute, hence when he told the congregation at Corinth that ladies should either wear a hat or have long hair in church, he was not necessarily speaking to all ladies in all ages. (1 Corinthians 11:5) This injunction may be taken as context-specific, although some Christians would say this is for all time.

- Research conducted through various branches of archaeology in the Holy Land, helps to confirm what Scripture tells us about the history of Israel. Consideration of the historical narratives discovered in the surrounding countries, have unearthed new information that may challenge some traditional interpretations of the Bible. Similarly, recent literary studies of the writing conventions of Israel and its neighbours have given reason to question the way we interpret Scripture using our own western ways of thinking.

- Then again, our differing cultures, backgrounds, and the context in which we live, can radically influence the way we interpret the Bible.

These factors help in part to explain the different thinking amongst believers, and also their particular ways of worshipping God.

How important do you consider the behind-the–scenes reasons for different ways of looking at things as far as unity is concerned?

....

....

- Sometimes the words of Scripture can be taken literally when they were not intended that way. For instance, 'I am the bread of life', a statement which should not be taken literally as the words of Jesus say, "these words are spirit and they are life, the flesh profits nothing." (John 6:63)

- The country's culture we live in dictates much of the way we think: for example, western Christianity will have different views to African Christianity. The mix of traditions with biblical concepts produces different emphases that can cause disunity.

- There can be disagreement through methods used to bring the gospel.

- Criteria for judging new insights can be a constant source of dissension. Prophecy and revelation are still given by God to His people today, but how to judge the truth of these things can be open to question. The Bible should be the final arbitrator, but with all the problems listed above this is not always straightforward.

- The different practices found in different types of churches. For example, some believers will only attend certain churches where new methods of worship are practised. Here, this could cause an unspoken superiority in those who think they have a mandate from

God on contemporary worship, and that any other forms of worship are unspiritual and outdated. Equally there are those who look down on all present-day worship styles as superficial and worldly, and allows no place at all for change. It is these two extremes that can cause disunity, especially when these varying views are held within a local church. People may have genuine reasons for not enjoying modern worship songs, just as there may be real reasons for not enjoying old fashioned, wordy hymns. The important thing to remember for those leading is that they are there to aid all in worshipping God together. Care and consideration for all who are in attendance should be encouraged as all are there as a body of believers to express their love, thankfulness, praise and devotion to God.

Knowing the factors that make people think differently may bring understanding as to what others believe and why they believe the way they do. This may enable us to change any wrong reasoning we have and recognise that there may be a better way of doing things.

Weakness

Satan is a master of dividing and destroying, hence the strengths of some believers can be the downfall of the weak.

In the Greek, to 'be weak' means to be without strength, to be powerless, to be poor, not having much faith. Romans 14:1 tells us to accept the person who is weak in faith, in this context it is referring to the believer who did not have faith enough to step outside of Jewish law. In fact, he seemed so scared of breaking the law he would only eat vegetables, as this averted the possible error of eating certain meats. These people were believers who so wanted to do the right thing, that Paul does not rebuke them, but rather calls them 'weak' in faith.

However, Paul had reached a place where he could eat meat offered to idols as it now held no condemnation for him as it did when he was under the Law. He was now walking in faith and was free from the old laws concerning eating meat, believing that God had given him the right to eat anything He had declared clean. (Acts 10:15).

Satan can put a tangled rope (stumbling block) between believers in areas like this, and can ultimately destroy their faith (Romans 14:15). Hence Paul tells the strong believer not to judge the weak believer to be inferior because he lives according to his conscience (Romans 14:22-23). He also tells the weak believer not to judge the strong believer as being in error (Colossians 2:16-17). Each stands or falls as their conscience dictates before their Lord.

How willing are you to step down from your freedom to believe in order to retain unity with a weak brother or sister?

....

....

St. Paul and Unity

In Philippians 2:1-4 Paul had reason to urge the Philippians to know how to deal with contention in the church (tangled ropes), as there was conflict between two women, Euodia and Syntyche (4:2) which was affecting the church.

"If therefore there is any encouragement in Christ, if there is any consolation of love, if there is any fellowship of the Spirit, if any affection and compassion, make my joy complete by being of the same mind, maintaining the same love, united in spirit, intent on one purpose. Do nothing from selfishness or empty conceit, but with humility of mind let each of you regard one another as more important than himself, do not merely look out for your own interests, but also for the interests of others."

Paul was making an appeal for unity based on Christ's example of humility and sacrifice. In the love of Christ and the fellowship of the Holy Spirit there should be unity of purpose in wanting to serve the Lord with affection and compassion. This doesn't mean that Christians are expected to think and act alike. While we are definitely expected to agree on the fundamentals of the Christian faith, there may be many minor matters of opinion that we may not agree upon. Where there is no real principle involved, we should back down for the good of others. We should have the mind of Christ and see things as Christ would see them. We need to show the same love to others as the Lord has shown to us. We need to be joined together in harmony, intent on one purpose, in order to reach the common goal. Paul tells us to do nothing from selfishness (desire to be No. 1, self-interest) and conceit (pride, self-display). Both are great enemies of unity and will stir up bad feeling and conflict.

The remedy is found in humility; to regard others as more important than ourselves. We should live for others unselfishly and consider others interests as well as our own. This is not natural to the human mind. We can't do this in our own strength but only in the power of the Holy Spirit. We are to consider ourselves servants of God and of others.

Sadly, there will be times when a dispute will end in separation as happened with Paul, Barnabus and Mark. (Acts 15:37-40) Barnabus wanted his cousin Mark to come with them on the second missionary journey. Paul remembered how Mark had deserted them in Pamphylia and clearly didn't trust that this would not happen again. The dispute became so heated and so serious that these two honoured servants of God, who were but ordinary men, parted company. Barnabus took Mark to Cyprus, Paul chose Silas and went through Syria and Cilicia strengthening the churches.

The question may arise, "Who was right and who was wrong?" There was probably fault on both sides. However, it was Paul who was committed by the brethren to the grace of the Lord. Clearly there was no lingering bitterness allowed to cause trouble (Hebrews 12:15) and though we don't hear any more about Barnabus, happily we learn that Mark was returned to Paul's confidence eventually.

(2 Timothy 4:11)

What do we need to learn from all this?

We should not be led by our pride, or our passions, or our natural or family affections.

Don't allow unforgiveness and bitterness to embed itself in our hearts when there has been serious conflict and separation has occurred. Make sure we are open and honest with God on the stand we have taken, and commit ourselves to the grace of God to direct our lives in accordance with His will.

God Himself will deal with any erring brother or sister. In His omniscience, He will work all things together for good. The Lord knows in time, if possible, restoration will take place.

Ultimately the unconditional love of Christ, which we as born-again believers have experienced in our own forgiveness and acceptance, must be evident in our lives to others. Love cements us together. Where there is this love, there is unity, and where there is unity, there is the Lord's blessing. (Psalm 133:1,3)

Paul endeavoured to deal with all sorts of tangled ropes, different problems that were the cause of division inside the churches he wrote to. He wrote to the church at Corinth: "Now I exhort you, brethren, by the name of our Lord Jesus Christ, that you all agree, and there be no divisions among you, but you be made complete in the same mind and in the same judgment." (1 Corinthians 1:10) He wrote to other churches along the same lines. His call for unity within a local fellowship is still the case today.

What possible reactions can there be when serious differences surface within the local church?

....

....

Upon what basis does Paul appeal for the unity of the people of God ?

....

....

Why? ....

.... (1 Corinthians 1:11-12)

What Jesus said about unity

Jesus wrote concerning the longings of His heart: "...That they may all be one; even as Thou, Father art in Me, and I in Thee..." (John 17:21) This is not a unity of doctrine or denominational aspect. It is not the unity of similar interpretation, or like-minded practice. Rather it is the unity that comes from being one in Christ. Just as the Father and the Son are of the same nature, so all true believers should exhibit the nature and behaviour of Christ. It is the picture of the vine John writes about in 15:1-10, where we are to let the life of Christ flow though us.

Can there be true unity any other way?

....

....

Why is our unity so important to God? (John 17:23)

....

....

Perhaps this chapter, describing the various tangled ropes we may encounter within the Church, may make us consider the consequences before we contribute to the disunity and disharmony that has so often caused God's people to stumble, and in doing so, has probably done serious damage to our witness to the world. We should always remember, united we stand, divided we fall.

"Therefore, since we have so great a cloud of witnesses surrounding us, let us lay aside every encumbrance, and the sin which so easily entangles us, and let us run with endurance the race that is set before us, fixing our eyes on Jesus, the author and perfecter of faith." (Hebrews 12:1-2a)

Chapter 5

Coping with Crisis

Which of the following responses would you have should a crisis occur in your life?

- Go straight to God and His Word
- Go straight to a confidant
- Panic, dwell on it, then go to God
- Make strategies for dealing with the problem
- Other

Isaiah 7:1-17 records this historical account of God's people facing disaster.

Israel and Judah had spilt into two separate states, but both made up the Israelite nation, chosen of God. Ahaz was king of Judah, and he ruled from Jerusalem. Israel and Syria had made a coalition to stand against the threat of invasion by Assyria. They wanted Judah to join with them, but Ahaz refused, so Pekah king of Israel and Resin king of Syria decided to compel Judah's co-operation by invading her and putting their own puppet king on her throne.

Ahaz and the people of Judah shook with fear when they heard that Israel and Syria were preparing to invade them. God spoke to Ahaz and Judah by means of Isaiah the prophet. He promised that none of their scheming would succeed. God commanded them to "Take care, fear not, remain calm and not be fainthearted." Their plan would not come to pass. Indeed within 65 years Israel will have ceased to be." (Isaiah 7:4, 8)

Ahaz was very scared, so God gave him all these reassurances, but still God had to warn him, that if he would not believe the Word of God he would not last.

God knew that Ahaz's fear of invasion by Syria and Israel made him want to control the situation his own way, so He offered to give him a significant sign in order to strengthen his faith. However, Ahaz wasn't prepared to believe God's word because he had his own agenda, and deceitfully refused God's offer of a sign, making the excuse that he did not want to test God. He was not as afraid of Assyria as were Syria and Israel, rather Ahaz wanted to protect himself by aligning himself with Assyria. (2 Kings 16:7, 8) If he had accepted the sign offered by God, he would have been under the necessity of believing that what God had said would come to pass, and this would have prevented him from doing what he was planning to do.

But God was not deceived and gave a sign anyway that pointed to a time of suffering for Judah, and would extend to circumstances far beyond the time of Ahaz, that would bring to a climax the prophecies and promises relating to "the house of David". Ahaz and the unfaithful like him, would forfeit sharing in the blessings of the fulfilment of the sign. He would not believe, and so turned to Assyria for help.

The three main Hebrew characters in this story are:

- King Pekah of Israel
- King Ahaz of Judah
- Isaiah the prophet

These could be paralleled with three factions in the Church today, each responded differently to the time of crisis.

The crisis in this instance was imminent invasion.

The Church is facing a similar crisis today, in that it is gradually being invaded by worldly forces.

God chose the Hebrew language for His people. This language is based on pictures, and often the meanings of names in particular, tell us something about the person or place they refer to.

Pekah means 'open-eyed, clear-sighted', and Israel means, 'he will rule as God'.

When a person becomes a Christian, God opens their spiritual eyes. This means they can experience God as the One who will care for and fight for His people. Israel as a nation had had their eyes opened, but they had sunk back into their old ways, and thought they did not need God anymore, hence they ruled themselves. They aligned themselves with King Resin of the land of Syria, which in the Hebrew means 'delight, satisfaction, pleasure.'

Pekah and Israel had become rather like the part of the Church which rules itself rather than relying on the wisdom of God and uses worldly strategies for its success.

Worldly thinking is a deception, it promises delight, and a safety-net to the believer but is not in line with God's Word.

The world impacts on the Church when it looks to powerful marketing strategies used by successful businesses, in order to apply them to updating its perceived old-fashioned negative image, with a view to better "selling" of the gospel to an unsaved world.

Can you relate any instances where you see the Church today being influenced by worldly practices?

....

....

Paul wrote, "We walk by faith, not by sight."

When we walk by sight, we judge situations by what we see and by how we feel. God wants us to judge situations by faith, by the direction He gives us through His word.

"Trust in the Lord with all your heart and do not lean on your own understanding. In all your ways acknowledge Him and He will make your paths straight." (Proverbs 3:5, 6)

Ahaz means 'to become a possessor of something',

What then did Ahaz want to possess?

- The acceptance and alliance of Judah by Assyria.

- He wanted to own the acclaim of Yahweh, God of Judah, but to work by his own rules.

Ahaz may be equated to the part of the Church that wants to have acceptance and help from the world.

These people like to be identified as Christians but God's power in their lives is restricted. Their God is confined to a box to which they hold the key. They limit His power. They make excuses for not trusting God, for when trouble comes and their lives are threatened in some way (e.g. their health, their business, their comfort zone etc.), they would rather look to the world to solve their problems.

Such believers sometimes find it hard to let go of their control of a troublesome situation and allow God to take the driving seat, maybe because of fear and unbelief, or maybe because they think they have their own perfect solution and as such, don't need God, which could be compared to thinking they know better than God. And perhaps if they achieve success through their own abilities, will cause them to continue to dominate and control situations.

Does fear make you want to take the reins of a distressing situation, rather than waiting for God?

....

....

Do you find it easy to trust God and let Him take charge when crises arise in your life?

....

....

Do you make excuses for choosing to do what you want to do, to get what you want, rather than allowing God to direct what you should do?

....

....

Do you have controlling and dominating instincts?

....

....

Does this effect your heeding of God's word?

....

....

Isaiah means 'Yahweh has saved,' or further, it can mean to 'be open, free and to bring salvation'. It refers to the work of a saviour, one who gets the victory.

Jesus was such a man who sought the favour of God and not of man. He overcame, and we are to be like Him. Jesus came purely to do God's will.

Isaiah, like Jesus, wanted to do God's will.

He faithfully brought God's Word into a frightening situation. He did not try to compromise or try to make it more palatable.

He was fully obedient to all of God's instructions.

To summarize, there are three types of believers highlighted in this story:

- Believers who have experienced God's care and protection, but have returned to the old ways, because they still hanker after the pleasures of this world, for that is what delights and satisfies them. They are not really loyal to God at all, or brothers and sisters in Christ, often preferring the company and advice of worldly people, and happy to rule themselves, though they call themselves Christians, followers of Christ.

- Believers who are fearful and fainthearted. They will only trust God for so much, as they are not prepared to fully work with God in difficult situations, seeking rather to trust in their own way of getting out of the crisis, instead of allowing and believing God to do what is right in the circumstances.

> Believers who live in obedience to the Word of God, and will trust Him no matter what.

Which of the above categories of believers would you place yourself in?

....

....

We see from all this that when we are not fully committed to God and His ways, we are deceived into thinking our way is right, but the natural outcome of our actions will not be good.

However, there are more troubles ahead for deceived Christians, especially when they are proved to be untrue to the One true God.

Chapter 6

Wooed by the World (spiritual unfaithfulness)

In the Book of James, those who have put the inordinate love of the things of this world in place of God, are considered to be spiritually adulterous.

"You adulteresses, do you not know that friendship with the world is hostility towards God, therefore, whoever wishes to be a friend of the world makes himself an enemy of God." (James 4:4)

Adultery

This can be both a metaphorical and literal sin.

Metaphorically, James calls believers who idolize the ways of the world 'adulteresses'. They have left the God they are supposed to love exclusively, for such things as money-making, the quest for power, pleasure seeking, reputation and anything else that panders to our love of self.

This makes us an enemy of God as we have traded the riches we have in Christ for the deceitful riches of this worldly life. He is a jealous God, jealous when He sees His children turn back to the very things He died to save us from.

We have to live in the world, but how do we determine what is acceptable and what is not acceptable behaviour to God, in a worldly context?

....

....

Is there anything you treasure, of worldly value that you would not be willing to relinquish to God?

....

....

"Instruct those who are rich in this present world not to be conceited or fix their hope on the uncertainly of riches, but on God, who richly supplies us with all things to enjoy." (1 Timothy 6:17)

The metaphorical meaning of adultery is clearly seen in the behaviour of wayward Israel as in Hosea 2:8. The god they honoured was Baal, the Hebrew word for Baal is 'husband'. Israel was meant to be betrothed to Jehovah, but their behaviour showed their allegiance to another. This shows to us that we can say we worship God, but in fact our lifestyle or behaviour reveals our spiritual adultery. The book of Hosea depicts not only the unfaithfulness of the Hebrews, but God's longsuffering, compassion and forgiveness. This was not however without God's righteous judgement on His adulterous people.

Literally, the seventh commandment says, "You shall not commit adultery." (Exodus 20:14). The world says it is acceptable to commit adultery if you are not happy in your marriage. Jesus taught that adultery was totally unacceptable to God, and was a sin which resulted in the adulterer being barred from entrance to the kingdom of heaven, if repentance was not forthcoming (Matthew 19:6 and 1 Corinthians 6:9-10). God hates divorce (Malachi 2:16), yet sadly it is as prevalent in the Church today as it is in the world.

Is there forgiveness after an adulterous Christian has remarried?

....

....

What is your reaction to the biblical teaching on adultery?

....

....

....

God alone knows the hearts of His people, He is a merciful God but there are consequences when we sin, He will judge His people.

Luke 13:24 states, "Strive to enter by the narrow door for many I tell you, will seek to enter and will not be able." The Christian path is sometimes a very difficult road to follow, and sometimes it costs us our personal happiness. Jesus said to His disciples, "If anyone wishes to come after Me, let him deny himself and take up his cross, and follow Me. For whoever wishes to save his life shall lose it, but whoever loses his life for My sake shall find it." (Matthew 16:24-25)

Idolatry: The beginning of spiritual adultery

A definition of idolatry is that it is the worship of something or someone other than God, as if it were God.

The practice of Idolatry is witnessed in the behaviour of Israel, God's own covenant people, when they unfaithfully went back to the heathen way of worshipping deity. A case in point was when Israel was gathered before Mount Sinai and Moses had gone up the mountain to receive the Ten Commandments. The people grew impatient because Moses was gone for so long. They decided to make their own version of God, the god that they had control over, rather than having to wait for God to instruct them. They took matters into their own hands and acted as the nations around them would do. All the gold earrings were gathered from the people, melted down and made into a golden calf, and was labelled 'the god who had brought them out of Egypt'. They prayed to this god, offered him sacrifices and partied immorally. As a result, when Moses returned, God's wrath was against them and they suffered greatly. (Exodus 32:1-10) Over the years there were many examples of Israel's unfaithfulness. God saw these actions as idolatry.

The reasons for their unfaithfulness witnessed in idolatry were many, some are listed below:

- Fed up waiting for God, so they provided their own source of help and worship.

- They still thought and reacted in worldly ways, so they wanted to gratify the desires of the flesh and worship other gods for their particular benefits, hence turning their backs on God. (Jeremiah 32:30-35)

- Ungodly influences as in the case of Solomon in 1 Kings 11:4. His foreign wives persuaded him to worship their gods as well as Yahweh, the one true God.

- They were double-minded and wanted the best of both worlds. They wanted the benefits of being a nation under covenant with Yahweh, plus the benefits of foreign gods that the surrounding nations worshipped. The benefits offered to those who worshipped deities could be fertility, prosperity, retribution on enemies and an acceptability by those of the heathen nations who also worshipped these gods.

This is typical of the things that woo the worldly Christian today.

There are churches who are happy to compromise with ungodly sources in order to get financial benefit, and others who align themselves with unbiblical Christianity in order to gain benefits and acceptance from the community. All of this has ability to contaminate and weaken our Christian voice in the community.

Sadly there are those who don't wait for God to instruct them, they help themselves and do their own thing by using ungodly and worldly ways of worship to bring the world into the Church, but in doing so have succeeded in doing the very opposite.

Is there anything from the above list that you can personally identify with?

....

....

We are warned against our involvement in spiritual idolatry. In a mysterious way idol worship is linked to demons. Scripture teaches that when gentiles worship or sacrifice to idols, it is offered to demons who control those who worship them. When we indulge in spiritual idolatry (worshipping or sacrificing to anything other than God) we are allowing demons to control our hearts and minds.

(1 Corinthians 10:19-20)

The spiritually idolatrous Christian may condemn the sin of witchcraft yet be guilty of the same when blindly idolizing counterfeit leaders that encourage anti-biblical spiritual experiences that (if they have the Spirit of God) they may question, yet foolishly go along with.

Other believers may indulge in witchcraft when they follow a formula of prayer, where their so called 'faith', is effectively a mantra or chant to get what they want.

Involvement with the Paranormal

Some Christians may not even consider the following unholy practices to be dangerous, yet if they are not wise and discerning, can get sucked in without even realizing it.

It is worldly practice to seek answers to life's questions through forbidden supernatural means such as, astrology, Ouija boards, sorcery, clairvoyance, spiritualism, fortune tellers, tarot card readings and other such ventures, which all come under the heading of witchcraft. These are incredibly dangerous because any involvement by Christians in such practices can remove God's hedge of protection, and if fully indulged in, allows Satan's poison to enter us. "Whoever breaks through a hedge can be bitten by a serpent." (Ecclesiastes 10:8 KJV). The hedge that God has placed around believers are His commands in Scripture as to how to live our lives. We are kept safe when we do things God's way as we are following the Maker's instructions. The moment we decide to 'do it our way', particularly by seeking advice in the places listed above, what we are effectively doing is asking the devil for his intervention in our lives out of ignorance.

Having read the list above, the Christian might well think this does not apply to them. However, they can be involved unwittingly by watching, reading or listening to today's multi-media which contains much occultic material which has great fascination to the vulnerable, especially young people.

What popular Books, TV programmes/Films/Computer games, Music etc. do you know of that may be considered occultic and are explicitly supernatural or contain an element of this?

....

....

Do you consider these to be dangerous?

....

....

Why or Why not? ....

....

Hypnotism is used by many people who want to give up smoking, or something else that they feel they don't have the ability or discipline to overcome. It is also a popular entertainment used around the country whereby those in the audience allow their minds to become subject to external suggestion by the hypnotist, resulting in the participants becoming the entertainment. This may seem very amusing at the time, but when anyone, particularly a Christian, allows their minds to be open to the control of another, we give ground to the enemy of our souls to come in and wreak havoc. Many have suffered greatly as a result of this, (which the world will attribute to mental illness) causing uninitiated trances, terrible fear, hearing of voices, and worse.

The world offers many options to the relief of stress. These have become so fashionable that even Doctors suggest alternative therapies that have not undergone the rigorous tests needed to prove their worth. Many have their roots in different religions and are therefore not compatible with Christianity. Believers need to steer clear of such practices as Yoga, Reiki, Reflexology, Acupuncture, Homeopathy, and any other New Age teaching that, though it may seem to be effective, is a deception and an inroad into the occult.

The dangers of participating are varied, the use of mind control techniques, which can open the mind to evil forces, or the belief that there are life forces in our bodies that are energy channels that certain practices can tap into, whereas the Bible teaches that God is our only life source. (Genesis 2:7)   The practice of Acupuncture is based on the religious aspects of Confucianism, Buddhism, and Daoism, of which Christians should have nothing to do with.

One description of Yoga means the union of the human soul with the Universal Soul (Brahma). It has been practised by Hindu Yogis for thousands of years. In order to attain this, there are eight stages. The first stage is yama, restraint and self-control. The third stage is asana, or correct posture and the reduction to a minimum of all bodily movements. Through difficult physical poses, both mind and body are disciplined. In the West these stages of Yoga are used as a means of gaining self-control, relaxation and better health, but true Yoga is a spiritual exercise.

So, we see from this that Yoga is considered a way of salvation. Physical exercise cannot be separated from the mental exercise that is from the meditation. When a believer gets involved, they are taking part in the forms and ritual of the Hindu religion.

Christians that have been caught up in this practice have experienced difficulty praying and reading the word of God. Some have had out of body experiences due to passivity created by the relaxation exercises.

If Christians have participated in any of the above practices, they are guilty of spiritual unfaithfulness and, as with Israel of old, will bear the repercussions of their actions.

In summary, John writes, "He that is born of God keeps himself (from evil) and the wicked one cannot touch him." (1 John 5:18 KJV) There are different translations of the Greek here, but both are saying that being protected from the devil is conditional on the believer's remaining under the protection of Christ.

So what does it mean to be 'touched by evil'? The Greek word used here for 'touch' means 'to attach to for the purposes of manipulating'. In other words, when we, for example, seek illicit supernatural experience, we give the devil the right to contaminate our lives.

The Bible tells us involvement in such things is detestable to God (Deuteronomy 18:12), because we are no longer blameless when we choose to go down this route, even if we are unaware of the dangers.

If anyone reading this has gone down the route spoken of and wishes to return to God, the first step is recognition of the wrong, and a genuine wanting to repent. "If any one confesses their sins, God is faithful and just to forgive us our sins and to cleanse us from all unrighteousness." (1 John 1:9) However, depending on the level of involvement in such practises, extricating ourselves from evil can be a very painful process. This is talked about in further detail in the chapter titled 'Squatters in the House'.

What experience, if any, do you have of the above practices?

....

....

Are there areas in your Christian walk where you are experiencing bondage in any way, e.g., difficulty in praying, reading the word of God?

....

....

Being wooed by the world is a major way that believers can be pulled away from God to follow their own selfish inclinations and ambitions, and as a result are actually, unfaithfully following after other gods. Therefore, it is vital that we recognise that though the temptations we face may come from the World and the Flesh, they also come from a malicious enemy who seeks to destroy our Christian faith altogether.

Chapter 7

The Enemy of our Lives

To understand how Satan infiltrates the Church, the lives of individuals and future events, we need to know more about him.

Here is a potted outline of the past, present and future destiny of Satan.

We are introduced to a serpent in Genesis 3:1-15. This creature is clearly Satan as referred to in 2 Corinthians 11:3. We read in Genesis 3:15 that his ultimate defeat shall come through the woman's seed (the Messiah) who would crush the Devil's head, (the wound administered at Calvary. (Romans 16:20)

In Ezekiel 28 specifically verses 11-19, although speaking of the King of Tyre, the scripture is clearly referring to the person of Satan. This is a similar situation to that of certain Messianic Psalms where the writer is apparently referring to himself, though it is clear that the statements and conditions can clearly also apply to the Messiah. (Psalm 22:1, 6, 8, 14, 15-18)

From the passage in Ezekiel, we are given amazing insight into the devil's attributes and functions. Although there was a human Prince of Tyre (28:1-10), who was very similar to the Roman Emperors of old who were perceived to be god-like, Ezekiel 28:11-19 clearly speaks of another, who was the King of Tyre.

He was created perfect, full of wisdom, perfect in beauty. He had the anointing of God to cover the throne of the Almighty. He was the chief cherub that covered the mercy seat. Here again we learn he was in Eden the garden of God, but he was clearly not seen as a serpent at this point. He was blameless until unrighteousness was found in him.

How can the description of the King of Tyre be viewed as a clear reference to Satan? (Ezekiel 28:11-19)

....

....

As a created being he was morally free and able to choose evil, but not obliged to do so. Although he started in truth, he became guilty of incredible pride by desiring and believing he could actually be like the "Most High". He sought to do this through counterfeiting the one true God. In Isaiah 14:12 his heavenly title was "star of the morning, or shining one, son of the dawn." The KJV translates it as "Lucifer son of the morning." He is the most superior being ever created by God without replicating Himself, whereas Jesus is the exact replication of the Father, but Jesus was not created, having always existed. It was only His physical body that was created. The New Testament shows us that Christ is "the morning star that arises in your hearts," (2 Peter 1:19) (Revelation 2:28), and Jesus is also called "the Root, the Offspring of David (which Satan is not), the Bright Morning Star." (Revelation 22:16 NKV) In Job 38:4-7 we discover that all of the angels are "morning stars," but Christ is distinguished as "the Bright" One. However, Satan is capable of counterfeiting Christ Himself as he comes as a shining one, "an angel of light". (2 Corinthians 11:14)

Indeed, there are some false religions and secret organisations that hold to an erroneous assertion that Jesus and Satan are one. They believe that because man is born in the image of God, he is both good and evil.

From this we can see just one of the ways in which the enemy infiltrates his deception to the world, that it is he that is God.

Where is he now?

In Isaiah 14:12-20, the prophet is looking backwards over Satan's whole time on earth, as much of what is recorded is still to happen, although is it referred to as past. This starts with "How you have fallen from heaven...."

In Job 1:6 Satan is among the heavenly beings still free to come and go in the earth. Also in the New Testament, in Luke 22:31-32, he still has undisputed access to God. We read in Ephesians 6:11-12 that believers wrestle against spiritual forces of wickedness in the heavenly places. So, we see from this that Satan has not yet fallen from heaven at this present time. In 1 Peter 5:8-9 and Revelation 2:13 it is clear that Satan has access to earth, but this does not mean that he has been cast out of heaven. We read in Revelation 12:7-10 that he was banished from heaven. However, the context of this scripture teaches that this will not happen until this prophecy has been fulfilled, just prior to our God setting up His Kingdom on earth and the authority of His Christ has come.

When our Lord said that He saw Satan fall from heaven like lightning in Luke 10:18, it must be concluded that this was a prophetic statement and not a historic fact. The seventy had just returned rejoicing that even the demons were subject to them. Christ's response was because He knew the mighty power that was yet to be displayed in banishing Satan and his hosts from heaven.

Although Christ totally won the victory over Satan by His death and resurrection from the dead, Satan is still allowed to reign as a usurper. This doesn't mean that there is a lack of sufficiency of power over Satan, it means that God's final judgements against Satan are not yet executed. It is only a question of when that sentence will be exercised.

Satan as Usurper

It still remains Satan's ambition to usurp the role of God with his own agenda, replicating and contaminating all that is good and of God. This includes the true Church, the Bible, through both wrong interpretation and misinterpretation, and also even diabolically counterfeiting the very trinity of God.

Satan is "god of this world" (2 Corinthians 4:4) imitating God the Father. In John 12:31 he is designated "ruler of this world" equating to God the Son. He is "the spirit that is now working in the sons of disobedience" (Ephesians 2:2), counterfeiting the work of the Holy Spirit.

This triune activity of Satan is seen throughout history but is particularly significant at the end of time.

Introducing The Antichrist

As Satan's ultimate desire is to be worshipped as God, his final attempt to bring about this deception will, to start with, be through a very convincing imitation of the return of the Lord Jesus Christ, in which all those who are unprepared will be deceived by the events that will surround this time, but especially through this person, the Antichrist.

Modern history helps us identify some evil oppressors whose characters typify this person. They were political dictators such as Adolf Hitler, Mao Tse Tung, Idi Amin, Nicoli Ceausesco. They all wanted to be worshipped. This is typical of the spirit of antichrist.

Scripture also reveals antichrist types for us. In Joshua Chapter 10 we read about a Canaanite king called Adoni-Zedek who ruled Jerusalem.

Interestingly the last time we hear of the king of Jerusalem (meaning peace) was back in Genesis 14. He was Melchizedek, a priest of God Most High, who is a type of Christ, the true King of righteousness and peace, and our Great High Priest (Psalm 110:4). However Adoni Zedek means 'the lord of righteousness', but He was a very wicked king and stood against the children of Israel.

It's helpful to realise that the devil knew that Jerusalem was a strategic area. Here Abraham had offered Isaac, but God had provided the sacrifice. It would be here that God would send His own Son to die for the sins of the world. Satan had had a stronghold in that place for the last 400 years. He didn't want to lose this ground and had therefore sought to establish his own antichrist Adoni Zedek, as king of Jerusalem, usurping and replacing the previous king with a king of his own.

How does this scripture typify The Antichrist?

- Andoni-Zedek sets himself up as lord of Jerusalem.

- Antichrist will set himself up as lord of Jerusalem.

- We read that Andoni-Zedek assembles five kings to fight against Israel.
- Antichrist assembles 10 kings to fight against Israel. (Revelation 17)
- In Joshua 10:11 large hailstones are thrown down upon the Canaanites.
- In Revelation 16:21 The Lord throws down large hailstones upon all the enemies of Christ.
- Joshua, with direct intervention from heaven defeats Adoni-Zedek and the Canaanites hide in caves (v.16).
- Revelation 6:15-17 At the time of Antichrist, the kings of the earth will hide in caves as God's judgement reigns down.

In Joshua Chapter 10 we learn that this was a battle like no other, as Joshua (also a type of Christ) leads God's people into warfare against this depraved king, who most certainly typifies the Antichrist. The reason this battle was so remarkable was that it foreshadows the phenomenal end time battle when Christ will come in judgement against the wickedness of mankind and will forever destroy this counterfeit Christ.

We read in Daniel 3:1-30 about Nebuchadnezzar, a type of those who deify man. He erected an image, and commanded that it be worshipped under the penalty of death. This is clearly symbolic of Revelation 13:14-15 when the beast of the earth made an image to be worshipped on pain of death. We have the phrase "The abomination of desolation" in Daniel 11:31 and also Daniel 12:11. Here the context teaches of Antiochus Epiphanes, a cruel tyrant and major antichrist type, who in the 2nd century B.C. desecrated the Temple in Jerusalem by slaughtering a pig in the Holy of Holies, knowing it was against Mosaic law. In Matthew 24:15 and Mark 13:14 Jesus saw "The abomination of desolation" as referring to something in the Temple at the time the Romans were about to destroy Jerusalem in 70 A.D. But the ultimate fulfilment of this phrase will occur during the great tribulation, a seven year period of time. (Daniel 9:26-27)

The word antichrist means instead of or against Christ and is only used in John's epistles although Paul refers to the same person in 2 Thessalonians 2:3, 8.

John tells us that the major way for the Church to identify the spirit of antichrist is to see where the coming of Christ in the flesh (God incarnate) is denied and hence complete Atonement through the saving work of the cross is rejected or ignored. (1 John 4:2,3) These people may profess to be Christians but teach another gospel.

Scripture teaches that the Antichrist, though he is not named as such in the book of Daniel (7:15-28) will come prior to the close of the age, before our great Lord and Saviour's return. Some believe this to have been fulfilled by Antiochus Epiphanes, but he did not fulfil all that was prophesied about this person. (Daniel 11:36-39)

He can be viewed as the second person of the 'unholy trinity' equating to Jesus Christ.

The Unholy Father

Just as God the Father was in the place of ultimate control working out His purposes through Jesus Christ, giving Him great power and authority as evidenced particularly in the signs and wonders He accomplished to prove He was the prophesied Messiah, so also Satan will be working out his purposes to deceive the world into believing the Antichrist is the Christ to come. Satan will impart great power, wisdom and appeal to this person, in his attempt to imitate the great return of Christ, as he too, will do many great signs and wonders (2 Thessalonians 2:9), amazing the world by possibly rising from a fatal wound. (Revelation 13:3) Scripture labels Satan as 'the Dragon', a very fitting title as the Greek word means 'one who fascinates', for it is he who deceives the world.

What do you think the attitude of the people of the world would be to such a miraculous leader?

....

....

The Unholy Son: His Character and Works

The ultimate Antichrist is the one who will claim to be the Christ, and is identified in various places in Scripture, revealing different facets of his character. He is called the 'Man of Lawlessness' or 'Man of Sin' (2 Thessalonians 2) His coming is marked by apostasy, a great falling away from the truth of Jesus as the Christ and Messiah. Many in the true Church will be deluded by him. (Matthew 24:4-5; 10-12; 23-26) This man is designated the Man of Sin or Lawlessness. This will be evidenced by his championing of new ideas and secular concepts; the beginnings of which are already seen today by the removing of the true concepts of life as written in the Word of God. These insidious views are already invading such realities as marriage, family, and the role of male and female. This also includes confusing that which is natural with that which is unnatural, hence diluting them into an anything goes scenario, and in doing so, weakening and destroying the most important aspects of society, thus violating the created order.

How do you see these issues evolving in society already today?

....

....

Initially the Man of Sin comes as one who seeks to unite the world through peace and prosperity. He comes as champion of all he claims to be good, but this 'good' is defined by worldly standards not by heavenly ones. And the world will follow after him. Hence lawlessness will greatly increase especially because Paul tells us that before the Man of Sin arrives on the scene, God will remove His sin-restraining influence (2 Thessalonians 2:6-7). There are different opinions as to what this restraining influence may be. Some believe the restraining influence to be the Holy Spirit as embodying the true Church, which is the Bride of Christ, thought by many to be raptured to be with her Lord at this time (2 Thessalonians 2:1). Others believe it to be the removal of the Holy Spirit from the World (Genesis 6:3a) but not from His Church.

If the latter is true, how can this be, since He is omnipresent?

....

A clarification may be given by explaining that in the sense that He came at Pentecost, a short period of time after the Lord's ascension, so too he will leave in preparation for the Lord's return. Although He is indeed omnipresent, the Holy Spirit came and was poured out at Pentecost even though He had already come upon the Disciples. (John 20:22) While it is thought He will leave the world in preparation for the Lord's return, yet still He will be in the hearts of all true believers who are still believed to be on the earth at this time.

The timing of the Rapture of the Church and removal of restraint spoken of above is questionable as some believe this event will not take place until after the apostasy and identification of the Man of Sin has been revealed. In this case it is thought to be between the sixth and seventh seal of Revelation. We don't know the day or the hour but it is thought Jesus will come for us in the night (Matthew 25:6, 1 Thessalonians 5:2, Luke 17:34, John 9:4). The night being a metaphor for great trouble. If this is true, it will be a very dark time of unprecedented tribulation for the true Church, as many will be martyred. If however we are raptured before the Man of Sin's reign of terror, the martyrs of Revelation 7 are thought to be the future subjects of Christ's glorious Millennium Kingdom on earth, and not part of the Church, the Bride of Christ.

The latter half of the great tribulation will be the time when peace will eventually be taken from the world, and war, famine and pestilence will come, as well as climatic and terrestrial changes. Great harm will come upon the earth, as the Book, sealed with seven seals is gradually opened. (Revelation Chapters 6-8) However, the Word of God will be preached by His witnesses and many will turn to Christ in the midst of terrible persecution.

Another name for the Man of Sin is found in Revelation 13. He is called the 'First Beast' who emerges from the sea. The sea in scripture often symbolises the Nations, therefore this person is thought to come from a Gentile nation. He will be allowed to have authority and great power for three and a half years, interestingly the same amount of time in which Jesus achieved His mission. The Bible tells us that all the people of the world whose names are not written in the Lamb's book of life will worship him. The Greek word for Beast means one who destroys, one who hunts the unsuspecting often by setting traps; what a fitting name for this malevolent character.

The Man of Sin is also labelled 'one who makes desolate' in Daniel 9:27 (see also Matthew 24:15). These names are particularly used in reference to his relationship with the Jewish nation, as he comes to desolate them. As we have stated, the Bible teaches there will be a time of great trouble on the earth after the coming of the Man of Sin. This will be an especially terrible time for the Jewish nation as Satan attempts to utterly destroy them, thus preventing the pre-condition for the Lord's return. It has been prophesied in Matthew 23:37-39, Hosea 5:15, Acts 3:19-20 that ultimately Israel as a nation must repent and recognise that Jesus is the real Messiah before He will come. This is part of God's plan and purpose for His chosen people which will be fulfilled before and after His great return. (Zechariah: 12-14)

Israel will initially be deceived by the Man of Sin as he will make a seven year peace plan with them, but alas his true colours will be revealed half way through this period, when he will have the audacity to take his seat in the Temple in Jerusalem, displaying himself as God. (2 Thessalonians 2:4) This leads us to understand that a Temple will be erected by this time, though not instigated by God. However, God will reveal Himself to His people and they will realise that the Antichrist is indeed a counterfeit copy, fuelled by Satan, who seeks for himself the veneration of one who is God. As a nation, and at great cost, they will repent and call for the true Christ to return. At the end of this period of history, though this man has been allowed to delude all those who would not receive the love of the truth, his end is determined, "the Lord will overcome with the breath of His mouth and destroy (the Man of Sin or the Antichrist) with the brightness of His coming." (2 Thessalonians 2:8)

The Unholy Spirit: The Second Beast

Just as the Holy Spirit is the Spirit of Jesus (2 Corinthians 3:17) and reveals Jesus to us, so with the counterfeit, the unholy Spirit will come as the spirit of Antichrist to reveal the Man of Sin to the world.) This unholy spirit is called the Second Beast, who comes out of the earth. (Revelation 13:11) The 'earth' here is thought to be the land of Israel, if this is true, he will surely be a Jew. He is thought to be a religious leader who will also be empowered by Satan to exercise great authority when he is in the presence of the First Beast. He will make the peoples of the earth worship the First Beast who received a fatal wound that was healed. The Second Beast will deceive the earth by telling people to make an image of the First Beast, he is also enabled to perform miraculous signs and wonders, even giving breath to the image. Hence, he is also called the False Prophet as he promotes the Man of Sin. (Revelation 16:13-14) Those who will not worship this image will be killed. The second Beast will be the one responsible for causing all to be given a mark on their right hand or forehead that will enable them to buy or sell. At that time those who have understanding will be able to calculate the number of this man, his number is six hundred and sixty-six. (Revelation 13:15) In the Bible the number seven is used to express the completeness of God or spiritual perfection. The unholy trinity may attempt to impersonate the genuine Trinity, but in the end, it is doomed to fail. Indeed, the number six has evil significance, which stands for the manifestation of sin. To the Jews, six had a sinister meaning, as seven was a sacred number and six fell short of it and meant failure. Whatever this may mean, the three sixes (666) are a trinity of evil.

Understanding of these things is partial now, but as the predicted time approaches, we believe things will become clearer until everything falls into place and predictions become reality.

These prophetic future events from Scripture which we have spoken of above are not taught much in the Church today. They may seem irrelevant to some, a lot of strange pictures that are very hard to interpret, which when they are taken seriously, can be interpreted in different ways, often causing dissension in parts of the Church. However, whatever interpretation of the end of time you may hold, we are warned by Jesus, not to be misled, but to be alert, for we don't know when Jesus is coming for us.

What is the danger of not being alert and ready for His coming?

……..

……..

Chapter 8

Deception of God's Children

The whole world is in bondage to the devil's rule and yet they are ignorant of his devices. Scripture tells us there are three sorts of people in this world, The Gentile nations, Israel and the Jews, and the Church, consisting of Jew and Gentile believers. The first two at the moment are deceived by their sin and are under Satan's headship, the third is now the target whereby he seeks to mislead as many believers as possible. (Matthew 24:24, Luke 21:8)

Throughout history, the spirit of antichrist has always been at work misguiding and deceiving. It is especially evident in our world today through its attempts to marginalise true Christianity. The spirit of antichrist, defined by John as those who deny that Christ is fully human as well as fully divine (1 John 4:1-3), is already at work through false religion, false teachers, and through false prophets who deceive people and seduce the apostate church, which is a copy of the genuine, in preparation for the advent of the Antichrist. Those who teach the Truth whilst denying and maligning it, mislead people from believing in the true Christ. (2 Peter 2:2)

There are many warnings throughout the New Testament for believers to beware of deception. Jesus Himself, when asked what would be the sign of His coming and of the end of the age, charged His disciples to, "See to it that no one misleads you" (Matthew 24:4). Babylon is the apostate church of Revelation 18. This harlot church is a vast false religious system which at that time will be a great commercial establishment as well, which apparently will control the world market. Sadly we will see that true believers participate in this subterfuge. God's people need to discern the corruption and deceit of this false religious setup and come out of her or they will be guilty of participating in her sins and receive the plagues destined to befall her. She is guilty of deceiving the nations with her sorceries. Her ultimate doom is inevitable, as God will avenge His martyred saints, apostles and prophets and all the righteous blood that will have been shed because of her.

The methods used against us

We primarily think of Satan as full of evil, the one who is behind the vile and disgusting deeds of evil we witness in our world today.

However, if he wants to be identified as God, what does this suggest about how Satan is actually wanting to be promoted?

....

....

The crux of the deception that finds its way into the Church is the lie that there can be godliness without God.

One of the ways Satan will infiltrate church culture is with subtle doctrine and practice that sets Jesus up as our most excellent role model, preaching that we should construct our lives as imitators of Him, asking God to help us achieve this.

However, the Cross is downplayed to the extent of it being unnecessary. In fact, in some Christian circles the cross is seen as child abuse of Jesus by Father God. These preachers say God can forgive without the need for Christ's substitutionary sacrifice on the cross. They reckon that Jesus died to show empathy with those who suffer at the hands of evil people.

Other so called Christian personalities believe that anyone could have died on the cross to shed their blood, and that Christ won the victory in hell by becoming a satanic being in order to overcome the sin of the world.

Look at the following verses and explain why the Cross is the only way we can be put right with God, made like Jesus and be set apart to live our daily lives for Him.

"Without the shedding of blood there is no forgiveness." (Hebrews 9:22) ....

....

"Being justified as a gift by His grace through the redemption which is in Christ Jesus; whom God displayed publicly as a propitiation in His blood through faith. This was to demonstrate His righteousness, because in the forbearance of God He passed over the sins previously committed. (Romans 3:24-25)

Paul warned about outwardly religious evil men who, "Have a form of godliness but deny the power of it." (2 Timothy 3:5)

What do you think this might mean?

....

....

When a person becomes a believer, they are 'born again' into a whole different life, into a different family, a different set of operating systems and a totally different way of looking at the world. They are born into the Kingdom of God.

Why do you think Jesus states that in order to become a follower of Christ you must be born again? (John 1:13, John 3:3)

....

....

Satan's deception says you do not need to be born again, you can work with who you are naturally and strive for excellence, and this is defined as being like Christ.

Paul wrote that we have this treasure (the revelation of who Jesus is, and the power to preach and live the message of the gospel) in earthen vessels, (2 Corinthians 4:7) so that the surpassing greatness of the power may be of God and not from ourselves. This makes it clear that the only way we can live and witness for Christ, is by the power that the Holy Spirit provides each and every moment of our walk with God.

Do you experience the Holy Spirit's power to enable you to live and witness for Jesus?

....

....

Satan's good news to the world is humanitarian in nature, talking about the essential goodness of mankind, whereas God teaches the inherent sinfulness of the human race. It teaches that we can overcome our failings through making the right choices, whereas God says, "apart from Me you can do nothing." (John 15:5) We entirely need His help, healing, forgiveness and guidance in order to make right choices, and to deal with the guilt and shame wrong choices may have resulted in.

Ultimately, he seeks to stop God's people from depending on Him for guidance and wisdom and get them to trust in their own wisdom instead.

He seeks to deter churches and individuals from actively living and recognising the fact that we live in the Kingdom of God. He fears the Kingdom of God will permeate our thinking. Jesus said this Kingdom, which is at hand right now, can only be seen and understood when we have been born again. It is a Kingdom of power, where miracles happen, where God is always at work intervening supernaturally, especially in times of crisis, strengthening and sustaining His people. God gives wisdom that is above natural thinking, (James 3:17), whereas Satan's wisdom is earthly, and sensual (James 3:15), wanting us to concentrate on natural resources rather than on God.

Hence it is Satan's tactic to elevate the natural over the supernatural. Indeed, one of his ploys is to ridicule the supernatural, this enables those that are fearful of such things to ignore or refuse it, as will those who are confident in themselves, and as a result they are happier to be reliant on their own control of a situation.

However, the opposite is also a great danger used by Satan. There are believers who attribute every supernatural occurrence as having come from God. This can come to those who earnestly but recklessly seek to follow the Lord, but do not know the spiritual world into which they are so blindly advancing. They do not realise that the fascinating lure of some 'signs and wonders' are actually the work of evil spirits. They think that because they honestly follow God, they will not be allowed to be deceived. Sadly, there are many that have been, and will be, deluded.

How is the supernatural perceived in your Church?

....

....

Satan does and will counterfeit miracles and supernatural happenings.

How then can believers differentiate between the counterfeit and the real, between lies and truth?

....

....

Firstly the counterfeit is clearly labelled in Scripture in terms of the conduct of such men and women who are inspired by Satan.

"For men will be lovers of self, lovers of money, boastful, arrogant, revilers, disobedient to parents, ungrateful, unholy, unloving, irreconcilable, malicious gossips, without self-control, brutal, haters of good, treacherous, reckless, conceited, lovers of pleasure rather than lovers of God; holding to a form of godliness, although they have denied its power; and avoid such men as these. For among them are those who enter into households and captivate weak women weighed down with sins, led on by various impulses.

(2 Timothy 3:2-6)

Secondly in terms of their teachings: there is a worldliness, a humanistic edge to what they teach. This deception may also contain the lie that panders to the idea that mankind is created in God's image and can therefore attain to holiness with God's aid. However there is a huge difference between when an individual appeals to God to save him, as opposed to one who appeals to God to help him save himself.

"See to it that no one takes you captive through philosophy and empty deception, according to the tradition of men, according to the elementary principles of the world, rather than according to Christ."

(Colossians 2:8)

Do you see any of these counterfeit teachings in your church?

....

....

Or somewhat easier to spot:

"……..Men who forbid marriage and advocate abstaining from foods, which God has created to be gratefully shared in by those who believe received and know the truth."

(1 Timothy 4:1-3)

However, Scripture teaches us an obvious way to spot the false.

"Beloved do not believe every spirit, but test the spirits to see whether they are from God; because many false prophets have gone out into the world. By this you know the Spirit of God: every spirit that confesses that Jesus Christ has come in the flesh is from God; and every spirit that does not confess Jesus, is not from God; and this is the spirit of antichrist, of which you have heard that is coming, and now it is already in the world."
(1 John 4:1-3)

This passage pinpoints the test for error. However, this does not excuse us from testing all teaching, interpretations, prophecies, and experiences against the Word of God. If they conflict with the truth of Scripture, they must not be believed. The Bible is the inerrant Word of God, but our cultural background can also wrongly affect the way we interpret it.

As a result of this, there will be different ways of looking at Biblical truth. It is therefore important that when we interpret the Word of God, we incorporate the the rules and principles of interpreting biblical text necessary to bring us to a right understanding of Scripture.

An essential test for validation, when seeking biblical understanding, is making sure that the meaning we attach to the words of scripture coheres with its immediate surroundings, and we take into account the 'context', the wider meaning of both the chapter and book in which it is contained. When seeking discernment, we also need to consider the literal or non-literal meaning of the passage. We must also take into account the historical and evidential setting to confirm the meaning we attach to it. It is best understood when one is familiar with the customs, culture, and historical context of bible times. (Luke 1:1-4)

All teaching we receive must be in line with scripture. The Holy Spirit illuminates and reveals God's truth to us, it will never be more than what is already written. And finally, there must be scriptural harmony. Individual passages of scripture must always harmonise with their context in scripture as a whole. We can never interpret a text in such a way as to conflict with other passages. God does not contradict Himself, therefore if a particular passage can be interpreted several ways, it must be interpreted in a way that harmonises with the rest of scripture.

Finally, another test for proving the soundness of a person or ministry is in terms of the fruit that is produced. Scripture teaches the principle of 'a bad tree cannot bear good fruit' (Matthew 7:15-20), for it is by their fruits we shall know whether they are good or bad. This will be evident by the lifestyle that they live and the things that they say, and it will not line up with the truth of scripture.

Good fruits are described in terms of righteousness or being imitators of Christ. We cannot produce this fruit ourselves; it comes naturally as a result of our life in communion with Christ. (John 15:5) Bad fruit is described in terms of unrighteousness or lawlessness. Sinners practice sin, and behave in ways that reveal the true substance of what they are made. (1 John 3:4)

Timothy makes it plain that believers should be able to discern deceivers. He writes: "But they will not make further progress; for their folly will be obvious to all." (2 Timothy 3:9)

Sadly, there are many naive Christians, who are all too willing to part with their hard-earned money to support these ruthless charlatans. These so-called prophets, prophecy many things that don't come to pass, yet this doesn't stop their often impoverished followers from supporting them in their lavish lifestyle due to the people's quest for blessing.

The believer who is following God will be tempted in various ways, especially where they are vulnerable, emotionally or spiritually.

Perhaps a major way Satan gets victory over us is by feeding us lies. When we believe a lie, we empower Satan and give him right over us in the area where the lie has been believed. He uses situations where, for instance, our prayers for deliverance of a long-term troublesome problem are not yet answered with the lie, 'God won't or can't sort your problem, and you're stuck with it.' If we believe this, he can then begin to feed our doubt with more lies about God or ourselves, and these become his building blocks for constructing a fortress or stronghold in our lives. Often the lies will nourish unstable areas in our Christian lives, our insecurities about ourselves or our faith. These poisonous lies, when believed, can have a debilitating effect on us, our relationships with others, and especially our walk with God, by creating such responses as anger, fear, hatred, worthlessness, hopelessness, confusion and condemnation. Most of all, if the enemy can convince you with his age-old lie, to doubt the power and goodness of God, he can rob you of the incredible victory Christ won for you. Our responsibility is to resist Satan and he will flee from you. (James 4:7)

Do you have any areas in your life where you suspect you have been believing the lies of Satan?

....

....

If so, be prepared to relinquish them to the Lord and allow Him to reveal truth to you.

Chapter 9

Defence for the warfare with Satan

Paul describes the way we are to combat the warfare with Satan.

"For though we walk in the flesh, we do not war according to the flesh, for the weapons of our warfare are not of the flesh but divinely powerful for the destruction of fortresses. We are destroying speculations and every lofty thing raised up against the knowledge of God……." (2 Corinthians 10:3-5)

'Speculations' are considerations and intentions which are hostile to the gospel: we are not to use those methods to spread the Word of God. Yet the enemy seeks to make us fleshly minded by looking to those things which the world uses to accomplish its aims.

The 'lofty things' that exalt themselves against the knowledge of God' is where the enemy has us looking at problems and crises from a very human viewpoint. In doing so, he seeks to make us doubt the power of God and His help, which is accessed through faith, prayer, and obedience. The enemy may also try to make us look to the proud reasonings of man, scientists, philosophers, evolutionists, or our own intellect, anything that is in defiance or disobedience to God. In these cases, we are to take "every thought captive to the obedience of Christ."

Since time began Satan seeks to make us doubt the true meaning of the Word of God by planting the idea "Did God really say". He also contradicts God's word referring to judgement for the disobedient, that the consequences of our wrongdoing are not going to happen. His motive is to make people believe that God's word is not true and He is not good, that He seeks to withhold benefit, and His word cannot be trusted or believed. (Genesis 3: 1-5)

Satan appeals to our fallen nature. James says that we are tempted particularly in areas where we really want to follow after an idea we are fed with, because our flesh desires it. (James 1:14)

In Matthew 4 our Lord was led into the wilderness to be tempted. After forty days of fasting, the tempter took full advantage of Jesus' great hunger by suggesting He use His miraculous power to convert stones into bread. To fulfil His natural appetite by the use of divine power in response to the devil's testing would be wrong. John classes this temptation as "the lust of the flesh" (1 John 2:16), which is not from the Father. Jesus only did what His Father showed Him (John 5:19) and His Father had given Him no such instruction.

For us, the tempter's equivalent temptation would be to get us to choose a way of comfort rather than seeking the Kingdom of God and His righteousness, thus succeeding in getting us to gratify our natural desires.

Have you ever been tempted to choose a more comfortable way rather than doing what was right in God's sight?

....

....

What way did you choose?

....

....

The tempter tried to get Jesus to demonstrate that He was the Messiah by performing a miraculous exploit. Had he succeeded he would have caused Jesus to achieve personal glory, but in disregard for God's will. This equates to "the pride of life". (1 John 2:16)

For us it is the temptation to get religious prestige, to make a name for ourselves, but not by aligning ourselves with the fellowship of His suffering. By this we ignore God's will and put God to the test.

(Matthew 4:7)

Have you ever tested God by participating in a spiritual exploit that you were not sure was in accordance with His will?

....

....

In his third endeavour to tempt Jesus, the devil showed Him all the kingdoms of the world and their glory. This equates to "the lust of the eyes". (1 John 2:16)   Satan so desired worship that he was prepared to give Jesus his glorious realm. It was his to give (1 John 5:19), although we are assured that when Jesus comes again it will be as "KING OF KINGS, AND LORD OF LORDS" (Revelation 19:16), then the kingdoms of this world become His. (Revelation 11:15)

Jesus' response was clear, "Be gone Satan, for it is written you shall worship the Lord your God and serve Him only." Jesus had a mandate from the Father and would not violate the divine timetable.

For us we must beware lest we exchange our spiritual birth right for the passing glory of this world and be tempted to worship and serve the creation rather than the Creator.

This is a very real battle. Ephesians 6 describes it as a wrestling match that is at very close quarters. When we are under attack, not from our old nature, but from the powers of darkness, we may wrestle with torment of mind, with confusion, depression, heaviness, doubts and fears, with evil thoughts, with bitterness and unforgiveness, which comes from the suggestions we are being fed. These temptations may seem so strong and forceful they will swallow us up. We need to recognise that more often than not, these thoughts are not our own, but are the inspiration of spiritual forces of wickedness that seek to impress them upon us. When we truly realise this, and stand against the attack, it will be a major factor in freeing us from their influence.

Do you discern when you are under spiritual attack?

....

....

Do you always recognise where these negative thoughts come from?

....

....

Paul writes that we are to take every wrong thought captive in obedience to Christ. We have the power to seize these thoughts and reject them. A helpful way of remembering how to deal with them is as follows:

Recognise   the wrong thought

Reject   the thought.

Repent   if it has taken hold and caused us to sin.

Replace it with the word of God. Ask God to give a scripture that will enable you to respond the way He wants you to.

As we bring the situation to God's attention, He brings His light and truth.

Do you manage to take your wrong thoughts captive?

....

....

We must realise that in our own strength we are no match for the devil. We are to be strong in the Lord and take on His power and ability by actively putting on the protective armour He has provide for us.

Paul writes to say we are to stand firm against these forces of evil. It is not flesh and blood we are up against, although we need to recognise that our opponents may often be human, but are unwitting instruments of a hierarchy of wickedness, that seeks to destroy our faith by obstructing and hindering our Christian walk where ever possible. That is why we need the boundless resources that only God's might can provide.

Let us go through the armour of God (Ephesians 6:10-18) and consider how these weapons can protect us from the attacks of Satan:

Truth - It is essential that we are faithful in keeping and believing the truth of God's Word, and that we apply it to our daily lives. If the enemy seems to be getting to us in some way and we don't know why, we need to take it to the Lord and ask Him to reveal the source of the problem. As God reveals truth to us, we can obediently deal with it, this removes the enemy's foot from our door.

Why is it crucial that we do not believe, or harbour lies in our lives?

....

....

Righteousness -This is thinking and acting how God would have us think and act. (Romans 12:2) It is also essential that we know that Satan has no right to condemn us. We have been given the righteousness of Christ, so that we may stand holy and blameless before God. (Ephesians 1:4)

If we are without offence before God, the devil has nothing to shoot at.

Peace - is what Jesus' death and resurrection achieved between man and God. As a result, those who belong to the Lord receive this peace as a permanent gift, but we must allow it to rule and reign in our lives. (Colossians 3:15) Also our feet need to be shod with the preparation of the gospel of peace. It's a state of preparedness to reach out to people with the good news of peace and reconciliation with God. It is also important that we have the peace of God for our ongoing walk with Him. The devil seeks to make us loose our peace.

How does losing our peace affect our warfare with Satan?

....

....

Faith - is a strong confidence in God and His word, and those who have faith, surrender to God's way of thinking and responding. The enemy can and will attack us in various ways. If we are not on our guard he can strike when we least expect it. He can use people, sometimes those close to us, to inflict great hurt by their words or actions. It is here that we need to be discerning and to recognise who the real enemy is. We are not to give in to our natural instincts to retaliate, but holding up our shield of Faith, trusting in God, we can then go on to pray and intercede for those who are against us.

We need to be prepared especially if we are going into an area that we know of, where Satan is active. It is then that we find great strength and protection in combat as enemy missiles fail to detonate.

What missile attacks have you experienced?

....

....

How does the shield of faith protect us?

....

....

Salvation - God has provided protection for our minds. It is called a helmet of salvation. We can assuredly know we are saved because of what the Lord has done for us. This helmet also provides the added knowledge that whatever we are going through, God will eventually deliver us. The timing and method of such a rescue is in His hands. It is therefore very important that our minds are protected against the wiles of the devil, since this is a major area of attack, and our eyes are on Him for guidance, especially as His way of rescue may not be the way we expect. The enemy seeks to rob us of the truth of our salvation, and feed us with the idea that God cannot deliver us.

The sword of the Spirit - This sword is the living and active Word of God. It is very powerful. The enemy cannot refute the truth of it. Therefore when we believe this, we may use it as an offensive weapon against him.

Our Lord showed us the benefit of knowing scripture and using it to combat temptation. Thankfully we also have the Holy Spirit to bring to our minds the Word of God.

We use it by asking God for verses of Scripture that we may use as a prayer, declaration, or code of conduct in any given situation where the enemy engages us.

Have you ever used the Word of God as an offensive weapon in this way?

....

....

What was the result?

....

....

We need to understand that "the reason Christ came to this earth was to destroy the works of the devil." (1 John 3:8) At the cross, the blood of Christ cancelled every claim Satan has against us. It has the power to redeem us from all sin and every lie of Satan, and by it "we have been delivered from the domain of darkness, and transferred into the Kingdom of His beloved Son." (Colossians 1:13)

Ultimately while here on this earth we are soldiers for Christ. We should always be on the alert. We don't know when that evil day may come upon us, but it will. The devil attacks periodically, so it may come when we least expect it, or we may go through a season of trial. This is permitted, that our faith may be tested and proved to be indestructible. (1 Peter 1:6-7) It is essential therefore to be in regular, if not constant contact with the One who enlisted us. It is He who guides, equips and establishes us.

As we seek Him every day, to study His Word, and pray, He will lead us and prepare us for whatever is ahead.

Chapter 10

Enemy Opportunities

Unfortunately, there are many casualties in our warfare with Satan, and though we know that if we endure to the end we will have victory, there are dangers ahead for those who reject the teaching of holy living and allow themselves to be drawn into sin.

What gives Satan the right to attack?

Sin covers a multitude of areas in which we give the enemy the right to affect us, because it is when we sin wilfully and break God's commands that we leave the protection Christ offers and open ourselves to be manipulated by evil. It is possible for evil forces to have a control in our lives causing great distress. But God does not leave us defenceless. True repentance and a return to God and His Word will deliver us from evil, though this may take time if an evil stronghold has been established. If access has been gained in some way, it may be necessary to have specific prayer for the casting out of these unclean spirits, but not necessarily.

As far as sin is concerned, if anyone refuses to trust in the grace of God by refusing to repent or give up their iniquity, the natural outcome is death. This may be physical death (1 John 5:16) or eternal death. (Romans 6:23)

1 John 5:18 tells us, "We know that no one born of God sins". John was talking about believers who do not continue to sin, that is, they have the divine nature and so they keep themselves, and do not go on practising

sin. In such cases "the wicked one does not touch him". He was not meaning that believers no longer have an old nature, and therefore do not sin. Indeed, John said at the beginning of his epistle, "If we say we have no sin, we deceive ourselves and the truth is not in us. If we confess our sins, He is faithful and righteous to forgive us our sins and cleanse us from all unrighteousness." (1 John 1:8-9)

Why does Satan attack?

In Genesis 3:15, God declared to Satan "I will put enmity between you and the woman, and between your seed and her seed. He shall bruise you on the head and you shall bruise him on the heel." This predicts the constant hostility between good and evil, between Satan's 'seed' (his agents) and the woman's Seed which was Jesus. The woman's Seed would crush the head of the devil with a mortal wound that would mean his utter defeat. This mortal wound was the result of the Christ's triumph at the cross. Satan in turn was to bruise the Messiah's heel, in so far as Christ suffered intensely in crucifixion and death.

Although Satan is a defeated foe, he is still allowed to prowl around the earth as a roaring lion, desiring to consume all he may, through the terror of persecution or any severe trial God's people have to undergo. (1 Peter 5:8)

Testing and Tempting:

The word 'tempted' means to test; firstly, in a good sense in order to prove someone good and acceptable, and secondly, in a bad sense of soliciting to sin, or of proving a person is evil. Temptation to do wrong comes from two sources. Firstly James tells us that it comes from within us: "Let no man say when he is tempted, I am being tempted by God, for God cannot be tempted by evil and He Himself does not tempt anyone. But each one is tempted when he is carried away and tempted by his own lust." (James 1: 13-14) The second source of temptation is from the devil, as in the Garden of Eden, when he tempted Eve with the forbidden fruit, in order to get her to disobey God. Eve's inward desires caused her to listen to Satan. At this point she could have said 'No'! In order for sin to come to fruition, there has to be an agreement between what the one being tempted wants and what the tempter suggests.

This suggestion of sinning, which comes from within man or from Satan, is the means by which testing occurs: the outcome is determined by the choices made to accept or reject the temptation.

The one who rejects the temptation, has proved themselves obedient and true to God. The one who accepts the temptation, has shown themselves to be weak and exposes the evil within them.

God does test or try people as far as their faith is concerned but never tempts anyone to commit any form of evil.

There are many areas in Christian leadership that offer hazardous possibilities, if one is not wise. The plan of the enemy is often to attack those in responsible positions of influence. In any war, if the officers can be destroyed, the rest of the army becomes vulnerable without leadership and this can cause the troops to scatter. Hence those in Christian leadership particularly need to be on their constant guard against the enemy, because if the enemy is able to make them fall, this will not only have a detrimental effect on themselves but also on their Church and especially on the weaker members of their congregation, possibly even causing them to lose their faith.

In what areas can our leaders be vulnerable?

....

....

In what ways can we be instrumental in preventing and protecting our leadership from enemy attack?

....

....

Root causes of spiritual destruction

The attacks of Satan can come on a sliding scale from the merest temptation, to a full-blown devouring of the person who opens doors to the enemy. (1 Peter 5:8) The devil's desire is to devour the believer through whatever means he can, be it persecution or deception.

Is this a warning to be on our guard, or is it a real possibility?

....

....

John wrote that "My Father, who gave them to Me, is greater than all; and no one is able to snatch them out of the Father's hand." (John 10:29)

Do you think it possible that Christians can lose their salvation?

....

....

Does this verse contradict 1 Peter 5:8?

....

....

"Many are called, but few are chosen" (Matthew 22:14): this verse indicates that not all who start as Christians will finish the course, as is explained in the 'Parable of the Sower' (Matthew 13:18-23), only those whom God chooses (1 Peter 1:1-2), (not that God 'chooses anyone for destruction') (1 Timothy 2:4). The 'chosen' or the 'elect' effectively, are those whom God knows will make it to the end of their lives trusting in Christ. Satan wants to prevent this happening.

The root causes of spiritual destruction are from the world, the flesh and the devil. Scripture strongly teaches us against being conformed to this world. (Romans 12:2) We need to be separated from it. Therefore, if we call ourselves Christians, though we may follow a form of godliness, but we allow our lives to continue in our old ways and act according to our unregenerated nature, then we sin and this gives ground to the devil. (Ephesians 4:17-27)

The Root of Apostasy

We know that before our Lord returns there is going to be apostasy, a defection from the truth. (2 Thessalonians 2:3) The ultimate aim of the enemy, as far as Christians are concerned, is to get them to reject the true faith.

In Hebrews 11 we learn of the heroes of faith throughout the Old Testament, who gained approval by God because they trusted in Him, and acted accordingly, despite whatever they had to go through. In Chapter 12, the Hebrews of the New Testament were being persecuted.

Read Hebrews 12:1-4. Why were they instructed to fix their eyes on Jesus?

....

....

5-8 Why is it important that we accept the various trials we may have to endure as discipline from the Lord?

....

....

9-14 What good do we gain through the difficult things His discipline will allow us to go through?

....

....

15-17 speaks of those who fall short of the grace of God, (perhaps never becoming real Christians in the first place), who have not kept their eyes on Jesus in times of trial or persecution. When trouble comes they turn bitter towards God and defect from the Christian faith, and in doing so cause trouble, defiling others in the process. (See also Deuteronomy 29:18) As with godless Esau, who gave up his birth right to gratify his appetite, apostates who willingly renounce Christ to alleviate reproach or suffering, will find it too late to reverse their decisions.

Chapter 11

Squatters in the House

Just as there are those who take advantage to squat in premises that don't belong to them and are vacant, demons use such circumstances to enter bodies when they have not been protected. (Matthew 12:43-45)

Demonisation

In the Church there can be an unhealthy over emphasis on demon inhabitation, that can cause great fear in some, or irrational responses in others, and as a consequence, demons are often classed as a taboo subject for believers, and therefore these problems are simply not dealt with.

The Church is divided over the issue, as some believe that once saved all demons must flee and cannot indwell a believer, however there is nowhere in Scripture that explicitly states that this is the case.

The thinking about demons in the Church at large, lies on a spectrum from those who would credit demons with causing every headache, to those who simply refuse to accept that Christians can have indwelt demonic problems.

We learn from scripture that the Temple of God had inner and outer courts and that God dwelt in the inner sanctuary, in a very special place called the Holy of Holies. When we become Christians, our bodies are called a temple of God (1 Corinthians 6:9) and our Lord dwells there, in our inner man by His Holy Spirit. Demons can have access to our bodies if we open our lives to what is forbidden, but they cannot possess us (own us) because we belong to God and He lives within us. These wicked forces may keep a person in captivity in the areas that that person has relinquished to sin. It is also possible if one has been a victim of evil, for example, rape, that the victim can give assent to a spirit of fear, perhaps of sexual intimacy, and thus unwittingly find themselves in bondage.

Ezekiel found detestable things and saw abominations committed by God's people in the temple in Jerusalem, both in the outer courts and the inner courts. This was the result of the people's idolatry, their taking part in and worshipping that which was forbidden. (Ezekiel 8:5-18) This provides an interesting, parallel picture of how unclean spirits can infiltrate our bodies and our souls because of our involvement with what is prohibited by God (i.e. abominable sin) However this parallel cannot be taken as doctrine, but as an illuminating example of how evil spirits can work in similar ways in the temple of the human body.

For example, if a Christian continues to watch pornographic material, they are opening the door of their mind to unclean spirits who will enslave them, so they cannot break free no matter how much they may want to. It has been said 'sex is a wonderful servant, but a terrible master.' Pornography is an evident evil, as are alcoholism, drug abuse, and any involvement with witchcraft. There are many non-obvious opportunities that demons can use to enslave, for example, when one has been exposed to rejection, perhaps in the devastation caused by the breakdown of relationships, when hurt or anger has been allowed to fester. This can then have potential to escalate to become a demonic stronghold of possibly rebellion, self-abuse, hatred and even murder. However, any area which has been allowed to have an all-consuming power over a person may result in demonic control.

Many Christians can still experience demonic problems today, which may be the result of sin or may be a hangover from their pre-Christian past, or may have been passed down through a generational line, especially if there has been occult practice in the family. These problems may not manifest themselves until something triggers them. It is then that believers may suddenly find troubles erupting that they have no control over, and have no idea how to deal with them. A case in point may well be when a person has been a victim of serious sexual abuse. This can be the cause of many oppressive issues in that person's life. Christian counselling and very possibly prayer for deliverance, may be of great help. In any problematic situation, in order to assess the need for deliverance, there has to be evidence of some kind that evil spirits have gained access.

Both the Old and New Testaments talk about 'uncleanness'. It describes that which is wrong and not how it is supposed to be by God's reckoning, and therefore it is polluted, defiled. Anything that is 'clean' is pure and is particularly useable by God. It follows that anything which is labelled 'unclean' may be used by Satan. Jesus and His followers cast out many evil spirits which the Bible translates as being unclean. (Matthew 10:1)

Any situation that can be labelled 'unclean' may give an evil spirit the right to become involved. If the demonic is involved, there will be an enslaving or controlling influence that will not go away and may well get worse over time. If the person concerned is walking closely with the Lord, then the demonic cannot comfortably co-exist with the Holy Spirit without there being a considerable battle. Sometimes God uses a brother or sister in the Lord with the gift of spiritual discernment to reveal that there is a demonic problem.

The matter should be brought before the Lord, perhaps in the company of a trusted, perceptive believer, to seek His light and expose the darkness. Then, if God so guides, pray for deliverance and cast it out in the name of Jesus. As the refining process of a believer takes time, so it can be with deliverance. Sometimes a demon goes immediately when cast out, and that is the end of the problem, but at other times, depending on the depth of the problem, there is a fight involved before the sufferer is finally free. The most important thing to remember in this battle is that God is sovereign and is in ultimate control, and that when we submit to Him and reject that which is afflicting us, we will be victorious. This may go on for a long time, even for years, as through this time God teaches His child vital lessons they need to learn! God loves His children, and though at times the process may seem unending and hard to bear, He will not bring full deliverance until all His purposes have been achieved.

Just as in Israel, the Lord did not immediately destroy all their enemies in Canaan (Judges 3:1-2), so the Lord seeks to make warriors of His children today using such situations to teach warfare.

There is great reward for those who have learned through battle. The final result will be a strong, faith-filled believer whom God has moulded to His specification.

So we see that though the enemy of our souls seeks to destroy us, God allows and uses all we endure for our good.

Chapter 12

Judgement Cometh

God in His grace and mercy has sent Jesus to deal with all the problems that this life has in store for us, His children. However, if we reject the help He offers through His word, we have to face the consequences of reaping what we sow. (Galatians 6:8)

Hilkiah the priest found the book of God's Law that had been lost. (2 Kings 22:8-20) He took it to King Josiah who read it and tore his clothes because he read of the wrath of God that would come to Judah, because they had not listened to the words of the book. As a result, Josiah was responsible for many godly reforms in Israel (2 Kings 23:4-24), however, the people's rebellious hearts had not changed. (Isaiah 57) Consequently, evil was coming in the form of exile in Babylon, and God wanted to spare Josiah the pain that that would bring. God chose to take Josiah out of this world to prevent him from experiencing the curse and desolation God would bring upon Israel because they had rejected righteousness and truth. Isaiah (57:1-2) comments that no-one sought to understand the reasons why God had taken a righteous man away, and that devout men who seek to make God's truth known are taken away from evil.

Today, Christians don't always read the signs that happen in our world.

Do we as believers ever question why there is no real clear Christian voice heard in our nation today as formally experienced?

....

....

Equally, God may allow catastrophe in times of serious crises. In His grace He warns us, but as with Israel of old, we do not always understand that God will punish us if we continue in our wickedness.

Do you see any such signs in our society today?

....

....

Do you see our nation as deserving of God's wrath? If so, for what reasons?

....

....

In Isaiah 57, God's prophet brought to light Israel's detestable sin of idolatry. In verse 9, the Hebrew word for king is 'melek', which can also be translated Molech, who was a god to whom the Israelites sacrificed their children, which was clearly an abominable thing to do. (2 Kings 23:10) From the context in Isaiah 57, adulterous practices with idols, transgression and falsehood were amongst His people. They had backslidden to the extent that they did not fear God (vs.11-13) but trusted in their idols who would utterly fail them.

Sadly even today Christians can still get involved with the things Isaiah was condemning for various reasons, some of them being:

- Ignorance of the Scriptures – Believing in supernatural phenomena that clearly contradicts what the Bible states.

- Naivety: Jesus told his disciples that they needed to be as 'wise as serpents', meaning that the devil's tactics are often subtle, and we need God's wisdom without which we will not to be able to spot the deceit. (Matthew 10:16)

- Idolatry: e.g. Idolising a celebrated Christian leader/speaker and his or her questionable teaching, rather than obedience to Christ and His teaching, making those who do so oblivious to possible error.

Would you ever be inclined to forsake conscience to be led by a Christian you greatly esteem, who is endorsing something you are not sure of?

....

....

- Wanting to hear what suits them: "The time will come when they will not endure sound doctrine, but wanting to have their ears tickled, they will accumulate for themselves teachers in accordance with their own desires, and will turn away their ears from the truth and will turn aside to myths." (2 Timothy 4:3)

Do you reject listening to Christian teaching that warns of trouble to come because it is unpalatable?

....

....

- Sacrifice of children: Today's society shows its lack of respect for life through its mindless slaughter of the unborn. Generally, abortion is chosen because it is an unwanted pregnancy, the result of immorality, or it is not beneficial to their specific circumstances at that time. Tragically, this is not confined to the people of the world,

Christians have also made these ungodly choices and without true repentance, will bear the consequences for their sin.

Is your heart open to deal with any areas the Holy Spirit has pinpointed in your life?

....

....

Reaction

When the Israelites had chosen the wrong path, they did not find it easy: it was a long, tiring route. Isaiah said, "You were tired out by the length of your road, yet you did not say, "It is hopeless." You found renewed strength, therefore you did not faint." (Isaiah 57:10)

This nation had seriously backslidden into spiritual adultery. Even though they were exhausted by their debauchery, they did not give up but seemed to get a second-wind and kept going in their deliberate wickedness.

It is the person who truly recognises their waywardness, repents of it, and turns to God for help, that will be heard and helped by Him, even though the road to recovery may be painful and the consequences hard to bear.

Why is 'sitting on the fence' not a valid option?

....

....

The Judgement of God as Natural Consequences (Romans 1:18)

- When God created man, He sovereignly planted evidence of Himself in each one of us, externally through the demonstrated power of the Godhead evident in what has been made in creation, and internally through our conscience, but in wickedness and irreverence mankind refused to allow the truth before them to affect their lives. In doing so they became destitute of real wisdom, preferring instead to live and act unrighteously, the way that ought not to be. Therefore, in God's great indignation He gave them over to the evil desires of their hearts and the natural consequences of their actions.

Can Romans 1:18 also apply to Christians? Why or why not?

....

....

Abandoned to the Judgement of God

Consider the story of Sampson: his life had been set apart for God, and God had used him as one of His mighty warriors. But he had a weakness, which proved to be his downfall. (Judges 16) So many times God graciously saved him from the consequences of his weakness and sin, but there came a point where God had had enough. The sad thing is, Sampson had ignored God and done his own thing for so long, he didn't even realize that the power of God had left him and he had been abandoned to his terrible fate. And yet, at the end when he had been blinded and imprisoned by the Philistines, God graciously heard his repentant cry and gave him the strength to kill many of his captors before he died.

The prime example of God's abandonment as a result of judgement is the people of Israel, who having experienced God's amazing grace in delivering them from their enemies, still turned away from God, refusing His powerful intervention. After being left to their fate, the Israelites came to realize their utter need of God.

In the book of Judges alone this sequence happened 13 times. Generations of Israelites would commit spiritual adultery with the surrounding nations. With no strong leadership after the death of Joshua, the people became disorganised and 'did what was right in their own eyes.' They repeatedly fell into idolatry, intermarriage with pagans and other major sins. As a result, God abandoned them to defeat and occupation by their enemies. After they had suffered significantly, God raised up godly judges who convicted the people of their sins. They repented and pleaded with God to help them. He stepped in and defeated their enemies, restoring their land and their relationship with Him. But tragically, after a generation or so, the people forgot how God had saved them, and the whole sad cycle began again.

In the book of Hebrews, the writer tells the story of the Israelites when they first came out of Egypt. They were guilty of disobedience, faithlessness and lack of trust in the God of promise. And God swore in His wrath that they should not enter his rest. (Hebrews 3:7-4:7)

Equally all believers are warned; "Take care, brethren, lest there should be in any one of you an evil, unbelieving heart in falling away from the living God... Let us therefore be diligent to enter that rest lest anyone fall through following the same example of disobedience." (Hebrews 3:12; 4:11)

Just as Jews of that generation would not believe the Word of God and were therefore prevented from entering the Promised Land, so backsliders who fail to believe in the grace of God and live by the truth of His word, will fail to enter the Sabbath Rest. Initially this is belief in the finished work of Jesus, and therefore following obediently according to God's Spirit as He guides our ways through this world to the ultimate Sabbath Rest which is heaven.

How significant is the Word of God in your life?

....

....

God's Eschatological Judgement

The prophets of the Bible foretell a time coming at the end of this world when God will pour forth His wrath on the nations of this earth in judgment of their wickedness. Yet even in the midst of His wrath, He holds out a loving hand to those who will repent. But judgement will come firstly in the form of the catastrophic events as recorded in Revelation, which include famine, war, destructive forces, plague, and deception by the Antichrist. We witness evidence of these hardships already, that at this time in our history are increasing, and serve as a warning (if we heed it) for the trouble that is to come. These will take place before the mighty second coming of Christ, it is then that the world as we know it will be changed. After this our Lord Jesus Christ will come back with His saints. (Revelation 19:14) He will rule in great power for a thousand years on this earth (see also Psalm 72:1-20, Is. 2:1-4, Dan.2:44). Sin will still be present in the world (Isaiah 65:17-25), though very much contained as Satan will be imprisoned until the end of this time. Scripture tells us he must be released for a short while. Then he will deceive the nations, and gather those who will not turn from their sin, to war against the Holy ones, which will inevitably end in their demise. (Revelation 20:7-10)

Our Lord's purpose for the millennial rule will be to fulfil all of God's promises to Israel, which could not be achieved without this future period of time. However His ultimate purpose is to eradicate sin and rebellion, and to destroy the last enemy – death. (1 Corinthians 15:25-26)

A Warning to the Church of Laodicea

What is God's warning to the Church at this time in history?

In Revelation 2:1 – 3:22 we read the chapters that contain letters from our Lord to the seven churches in Asia Minor. These letters can be viewed and studied in various ways. Many understand these letters to relate to the history of Christendom. Each church reflects a noticeable period that can be identified with each phase of it's existence.

- Ephesus: corresponds to the apostolic church. The first century church was generally praiseworthy but had left it's first love.
- Smyrna: From the first to the fourth century the church suffered great persecution under the Roman emperors.
- Pergamum: represents the state church, nominal Christianity that tolerated pagan practices, beginning with Constantine and continuing to the end.
- Thyatira: From the sixth to the fifteenth century, the Roman Catholic Church had influence over Western Christendom until the Reformation. The Orthodox Church ruled in the East.
- Sardis: The sixteenth and seventeenth centuries pictures the Reformation church. The light of the Reformation soon became dim.
- Philadelphia: This church has the characteristics of the great missionary movement, when there were mighty revivals in the eighteenth and nineteenth centuries.
- Laodicea: Pictures the church of the last days, lukewarm and apostate.

The name Laodicea means either 'the people ruling' or 'the judgement of the people'.

The church was neither hot nor cold. It had become Lukewarm, which is not palatable to drink, and which Christ would spit out of His mouth. The Laodicean church was also proud, ignorant of its true state, self-sufficient and complacent. There was great need for them to buy gold refined in the fire, which may mean that they needed to have genuine faith, which when tested "may be found to result in praise and glory and honour at the revelation of Jesus Christ." (1 Peter 1:17) This church needed to recognise its poverty and receive from Jesus righteous apparel, and also true spiritual vision through the enlightenment of the Holy Spirit. He calls on this nominal church to be zealous and repent. In the closing verses of this chapter we see that Christ is on the outside of this church, still desiring that individual people invite Him into their lives. "For the gate is small, and the way is narrow that leads to life and few are those who find it." (Matthew 7:14) For those who humbly follow their Lord, there may be suffering and rejection, but the overcomer is promised that he will share the glory of Christ's throne and reign with Him. The hearer is then seriously advised to listen to what the Spirit says to the churches.

Whatever interpretation we take from the book of Revelation, we can't deny that the church in Laodicea has very similar characteristics to the church age we live in. Many churches are ignorant of their true state. The undiscerning leaders bring a word that will not challenge or warn. And the people are happy, they hear what suits them. They are materialistic. They love their pleasure activities. They enjoy the pampering of self. They think they are successful, doing well spiritually, perhaps because of their wealth. They don't realise that they are poor, blind and naked, and badly need the Holy Spirit to enable them to truly see. (Revelation 3:17- 18) All these earth-bound things reveal a distinct lack of readiness for the eternal, and all this without realising the urgency of the hour.

What response do you have to this warning?

....

....

What is the remedy for those who want to turn their lives around in verse 18?

....

....

"...Knowing the time that it is already the hour for you to awaken from sleep; for now salvation is nearer to us than when we believed. The night is almost gone, the day is at hand. Let us therefore lay aside the deeds of darkness and put on the armour of light." (Romans 13:11-12)

This speaks of the need for the lethargic to wake up, because the lateness of the hour demands we have a change of heart, to get serious about our faith. The dispensation of Grace is coming to an end. The present night of sin will soon run its course. We need to remove ourselves from everything that is questionable and unrighteous, and put on the protective covering of a holy life.